Guaranteed CREDIT

A time-tested
program guaranteed
to provide clear,
step-by-step
information on how
to repair, restore and
rebuild your credit.

Arnold S. Goldstein, J.D., Ph.D.

Guaranteed Credit
By Arnold S. Goldstein, J.D., Ph.D.
Copyright © 1996-2002 by Garrett Publishing, Inc.

Published by
Garrett Publishing, Inc.
384 South Military Trail
Deerfield Beach, FL 33442
Tel. 954-480-8543
Fax 954-698-0057
E-mail: barbara@garrettpub.com
www.garrettpub.com

All rights reserved. No part of this publication may be reproduced or transmitted in any form or by any means, electronic or mechanical, including photocopy, recording or any information storage and retrieval system now known or to be invented, without permission in writing from the publisher, except by a reviewer who wishes to quote brief passages in connection with a review for inclusion in a magazine, newspaper or broadcast. Requests for permission should be addressed in writing to the publisher.

This publication is designed to provide accurate and authoritative information in regard to the subject matter covered. It is sold with the understanding that neither the publisher nor author is engaged in rendering legal, accounting, or other professional service. If legal advice or other expert assistance is required, the services of a competent professional should be sought. From a Declaration of Principles jointly adopted by a Committee of the American Bar Association and a Committee of Publishers.

Goldstein, Arnold S.
        Guaranteed Credit / Arnold S. Goldstein
        p.   cm.
        Includes bibliographical references and index.
        ISBN 1-880539-40-3 (alk. paper)
        1. Credit bureaus — United States. 2. Consumer credit —
United States. 3. Credit cards —
United States. I. Title.
        HG3751.7.G65 1995
        332.7'43—dc20   95-11997
                                                                    CIP

Printed in the United States of America
2 1 0 9 8 7 6 5 4 3

GOOD CREDIT GUARANTEE

W e guarantee that the strategies and techniques in this book will improve your credit to your complete satisfaction or we will fully refund the purchase price. This guarantee is upon the following terms and conditions:

1 The book must be returned directly to the publisher at the below address. Do not return to retailer. This is a publisher's guarantee only.

2 Return the book in resaleable condition and with the sales receipt within six months of purchase.

3 You shall be refunded the lesser of publisher's list of actual purchase price. (Excluding shipping and handling, if any.)

Garrett Publishing, Inc.
384 S. Military Trail
Deerfield Beach, FL 33442

President

ABOUT THE AUTHOR

Dr. Arnold S. Goldstein—America's *"Money Doctor"*—is nationally known for his innovative credit repair and debt management strategies.

As a senior partner in a major Boston law firm, he has assisted thousands of clients with their financial problems. He has also authored several books on credit including *The Complete Credit & Collection System* (Enterprise), *Getting Paid* (John Wiley), and *Commercial Transactions Deskbook* (Prentice Hall). Some of his other best-selling books include *Asset Protection Secrets*, *The Business Doctor*, *Debt Busters*, and *How To Settle With The IRS*, all available from Garrett Publishing, Inc.

His articles have been featured in over 350 magazines, journal articles and newspapers. Dr. Goldstein has also appeared on many radio and TV talk shows. A popular speaker on credit repair and related subjects, he travels across the country presenting workshops and guest lectures on these topics. In addition, he enjoys a distinguished academic career as a full professor at Boston's Northeastern University and has taught law, finance and management at several other colleges and universities.

Dr. Goldstein is a graduate of Northeastern University (B.S. 1961) and Suffolk University (MBA, 1966 and LL.M., 1975). He also holds a law degree from the New England School of Law (J.D., 1964) and a doctorate from Northeastern University (Ph.D. in business and economic policy, 1990). He is a member of the Massachusetts Bar and Federal Bar and numerous professional, academic and civic organizations. Dr. Goldstein enjoys hearing from his readers and can be reached at (954) 480-8543.

Table of Contents

How This Book Will Help You

Good credit is essential today. Without good credit you cannot get a mortgage, finance a car, obtain a bank credit card or even open a charge account at the local department store.

We truly live in a credit society. Much of what we buy is on credit. But good credit is equally essential even if you want to rent an apartment, lease a car or get a student loan. When you have poor credit—or no credit—you are forced to exist in a world where you must pay as you go. You cannot get the things you want but are limited to only those things that you can immediately pay for.

If that is you, I will help you change your life.

If you have *no* credit, I will show you how to *establish* credit.

If you have *bad* credit, I will show you how to turn it into *good* credit.

If you have *weak* credit, I will show you how to build *more powerful* credit.

But getting the credit you want won't happen without your commitment. It will take time—perhaps several months.

It also will take persistence. You can't always succeed in your first attempt.

Most of all, it also will take knowledge. That's where *Guaranteed Credit* will be invaluable. This is the book that reveals *everything* you must know to build or repair your credit. Here are all the no-holds barred secrets you need to survive and thrive in America's credit system—and get *all* the credit you deserve and can comfortably handle!

But there's more. I'll also show you how to:

- Get and read your own credit report so you know how others view your creditworthiness.

- Eliminate all—or most—of the negative marks or "dings" that destroy credit.

- Add positive credit indicators to your credit report so you build more powerful credit.

- Manage your finances wisely so you enjoy a lifetime of triple A credit.

- Win all the credit you need for those essentials *everyone* needs—a car, a house mortgage and bank credit cards.

- Exploit your credit to build wealth faster!

- Avoid the countless credit scams that plague America today.

- Save money on all your credit purchases . . . and much more.

Thousands of people from every walk of live have benefitted from the credit secrets I now share with you. Some never had credit. Others had their credit ruined because they ran into financial problems. Still others have had some credit but needed more credit to achieve more ambitious goals. More than a few are entrepreneurs who want more credit for their business.

It doesn't matter who you are or what your present credit situation may be. You can get more credit than you have today. I promise to show you how!

Will you succeed 100 percent of the time?

Probably not.

But you *can* significantly improve your credit if you follow my credit building strategies. In fact, I *guarantee* you will! That's why I offer you a 100 percent money back guarantee. If you are not completely satisfied with the results after applying my credit repair system, you get back every penny you paid for this book. But I'm not worried. I know *Guaranteed Credit* works because countless people have already successfully used my credit repair blueprint. Their letters tell me so. I also have heard their grateful comments by phone and at my nationwide seminars. That's why I say it can work for you!

The credit improvement methods you are about to discover aren't textbook theories. They result from the trial by fire that comes from over 25 years helping people to cope with their credit problems. I have learned, as you will learn, that our American credit system has weaknesses as well as strengths. Helping you to understand how you can exploit them to your maximum advantage is what this book is all about.

What you will find in Guaranteed Credit

Guaranteed Credit begins with an in-depth explanation of how our credit system operates, and the key role the credit bureaus play in compiling and reporting credit. You will learn how these bureaus really function as well as who is legally entitled to get credit information about you. You will then learn how to obtain and read your own credit report. You will then proceed step-by-step through the fundamentals of credit repair which will help you repair most of your credit report problems. To combat more stubborn credit problems is a chapter on advanced strategies to resolve such credit problems as tax liens, foreclosures, repossessions, bankruptcy, and judgments.

Once your credit is repaired, this book proceeds to show you all the powerful and proven techniques for building truly powerful credit. You then discover all the secrets of the credit card system and how to use that knowledge to obtain and wisely use credit cards. And to intelligently deal with the many types of lenders—from banks to used car salesmen—several info-packed chapters help you to intelligently use your credit to buy a car, a business or even a home.

Yes, here you will find all the principles of sound credit management. And they will serve you a lifetime and save you plenty of money. You will save even more money simply by avoiding the common credit scams that plague America today. I show you what they are and how to sidestep them.

But that's not all. *Guaranteed Credit* ensures that as a credit consumer you will never again be victimized. This book highlights the several consumer protection laws that protect your rights as a consumer and define the credit bureaus obligations to you. For example, did you know that if you dispute your credit report the credit bureau has only thirty days to respond—or it must delete the disputed item from your credit file? Or did you know that you have the legal right to include your version of a dispute in a written statement that must be attached to your credit report? Or did you know that you have the right to file a complaint directly with the Federal Trade Commission, or the Subcommittee on Banking and Finance, if your credit rights are in any way violated?

Yes, it's all here and even more!. But in addition to providing you clear, step-by-step information on how to repair, restore and rebuild your credit, I give you over forty sample letters to protect your rights in virtually any situation. These clear, concise, sample letters can be adapted or customized to fit your own special situations. Use these documents to help you pave the way to a powerful credit rating.

A final word: This is not a book about how to abuse the system, commit fraud or rip-off creditors. Nor is it a book about lying, cheating or stealing. It is a book about using all the legal tools that are intended to protect your credit rights—and how to use them for your maximum protection

So buckle up. Let's get you the credit you need and want in America's credit society.

April, 2002

Arnold S. Goldstein, Ph.D.

Deerfield Beach, Florida

Why You Need Good Credit Today

Why You Need Good Credit Today

1

How often have you heard someone boast *"I pay cash for everything"* or *"I never borrowed a dime in my life"?*

Years ago such statements were admirable. They implied that you had enough income to buy the things you wanted on a pay-as-you-go basis. With a solid income and sound financial management anyone could realize the American dream.

That was yesterday. Unfortunately, this is no longer true. Today we live in a credit world where serious debt, poor credit or no credit causes many of us high anxiety. Perhaps that's you. Maybe you too lack the credit you need to:

- Buy a decent car?
- Take a vacation?
- Get a home mortgage?
- Finance your own business?

If that *is* you, consider how much better your life will be when you transform your poor credit into excellent credit so these things can be yours. Let's get started. This book will help you do just that.

The wide world of credit

There are many different ways to borrow money, but only four types of credit:

1) **Secured credit** is credit backed by collateral. You pledge something of value to the lender so that if you fail to repay the loan the lender may sell the collateral. Collateral may be your car, jewelry, real estate, a passbook savings account or any other tangible asset that you and the lender agree upon. Because you have pledged collateral, the lender has the least risk, and so this is often the easiest type credit to obtain. A home mortgage loan, although less easy to obtain, is the most common type of secured credit.

2) **Unsecured credit.** The lender extends credit to you based upon your ability to repay the loan. You do not give collateral to back up the loan. Because there is no collateral with this type of credit, the lender has a much higher risk and therefore must have higher confidence in your ability to repay. Unsecured credit is mostly based upon your credit history and your current financial status. If you default, the lender must go to court in order to seize your assets and recover his money.

3) **Installment credit.** This type of credit can be either secured or unsecured. You are granted a loan or credit which must be repaid in payments or installments over a specific time period. One variation of this type credit arrangement is when your payments free up an equal amount of money which you can borrow again. For example, revolving charge accounts in department stores have a credit limit that automatically renews as you pay. Common installment loans are automobile, educational, and personal loans. If you fail to make timely payments you are charged a late fee. More importantly, it is reported as a negative entry on your credit report. Mortgage loans are also installment loans with the earlier payments on the loan primarily paying the interest.

4) **Non-installment credit** can be secured or unsecured credit which is repaid in one payment by a specified date—typically within 90 days. Any bill you receive that says "payment due in full upon receipt of this bill," is non-installment credit. A telephone bill or doctor's statement are common examples of non-installment credit.

As you can see, virtually everyone periodically obtains some type of credit. But regardless of your credit experiences, when you walk into a bank for a car loan, or try to open a charge account in a department store, your credit past inevitably follows. Of course, the one most important source for information about your creditworthiness is the credit bureau report. And your credit report will be taken at face value and quite seriously. It may be completely inaccurate, or even be someone else's report, erroneously bearing your name. Or it may reflect poor financial judgment from years earlier. Regardless, you will be judged and often quite harshly because of what the credit report reveals about you.

Good credit is essential to good living

Today's economic realities and business practices have transformed us into a cashless society. Cash is no longer king. The crown belongs to good credit. A point made earlier, the average consumer can no longer afford to pay cash for basic necessities, let alone expensive luxuries. Whether it be a car, a home, or a college education, all must be financed. This takes credit.

Good credit is convenient even when it is not essential. It is inconvenient and dangerous to walk around with large amounts of cash. Good credit, on the other hand, is invisible, weighs nothing and managed properly, is instantly available. You gain the joy of impulse buying. Good credit in a word, is power!

Good credit also measures your financial worth. It reflects your financial progress, character, and how others view your future prospects. Good credit also creates the financial leverage you need to borrow the money you need to build even more wealth. Lenders also see good credit as collateral, and they finance you based upon that collateral. For all it is, credit is only debt in disguise because credit must be repaid. Good credit also is confidence—the confidence others have in you. They give you credit because they believe you will pay. But good credit also builds your own self-confidence: You gain the confidence to plan, take risks, and compete effectively in the marketplace. And this is good for both you and the marketplace. Our society could not function without credit. Industry would grind to a halt and we would return to a feudal barter system. Good credit truly reflects your stake in the American dream.

Indeed, everyone needs good credit! As a woman you must establish your own credit. Whether married or single, good credit will help you build a positive, independent life and ease the impact of divorce, widowhood or financial setbacks. Laws such as the Equal Credit Opportunity Act (ECOA) are designed to protect women from credit discrimination.

Are you young? You too must master credit management and learn that credit is the foundation of real wealth. With credit you harness other people's money and other people's talent. Learn the credit basics when you are young and they will give you a financial advantage that will remain with you for the rest of your life.

Never lose your good credit

If good credit is essential for so many things, then how and why do so many people lose theirs credit? There are countless stories. Take the case of Ruth, a young woman who sought my counsel years ago after many unsuccessful attempts to obtain a mortgage. Ruth had never established her own credit and always relied upon her husband's. Upon their divorce, Ruth's husband used their jointly-held credit cards to run up $15,000 in debts that he never paid. These, of course, were demerits entered against Ruth's credit report without her knowledge. Ruth's divorce decree stated that she was not responsible for her former husband's debts and once we advised each creditor of the facts, her poor credit was corrected.

Leonard, on the other hand, was a hopeless credit addict with a weird but common philosophy: "My credit must be good. I owe everyone!" Credit-poor Leonard bicycled to work because he couldn't buy even a used car. Leonard was a perennial bankruptcy candidate. Without mastering the basics of sound credit management, the cycle would just repeat itself over and over again for Leonard.

Carl and Debbie enjoyed large incomes, but their fancy lifestyle consumed their every penny. When Carl was laid off their income plummeted 50 percent. Over Carl's 14 months of unemployment, the couple was forced to live on credit and they amassed a staggering $60,000 in debts. Even fully employed they had no hope of repaying. Their only answer was to modify their lifestyle with a strict budget. Carl and Debbie would only slowly rebuild their credit.

Credit can also be ruined by financial scams that anyone can fall victim to. Ask Tracy who owned a Florida condominium she could barely afford. Continuous assessments escalated Tracy's monthly payments from $500 to $900. When the condo. association assessed every household $11,000 for a new roof, Tracy was forced to take out a home equity loan with a local bank. Unfortunately, the roofer skipped town with the money. Unable to make the payments or borrow more, Tracy soon lost her property to foreclosure. Gone too was her credit rating!

Mike's new home also required a $900 monthly mortgage payment—almost more than what Mike could afford. Unfortunately, Mike never realized that his real estate taxes were based upon undeveloped land. The following year he was correctly taxed on developed land increasing his payments to $1300. When Mike couldn't find a buyer he too faced foreclosure and bad credit.

Carelessness is a common way to lose your good credit. For example, Donna could pay her bills promptly, but still paid late— often after she received a "final notice before legal action." Donna, victimized by poor recordkeeping, never balanced her checkbook, or knew about her bills, or even which bills she paid. And of course, Donna never set a budget. Her carelessness led to countless late payment reports which blotted and soon destroyed her credit.

Even one simple typographical error innocently placed on a credit report can spell the difference between good and bad credit. Not only must you learn the credit rules, you must also vigilantly guard against innocent errors that can destroy your credit.

Understanding your rights as a credit consumer

Before we advance too far, it is important that you understand your rights as a credit consumer. The key to repairing your credit is the *Consumer Credit Protection Act*. This law, enacted by Congress to protect consumers from unfair credit practices, also regulates credit reporting agencies, collection agencies and creditors. It also prevents credit discrimination and includes many other protective features.

The Consumer Credit Protection Act contains four important sections, all thoroughly covered in this book:

1) The Fair Credit Reporting Act (FCRA)

2) The Fair Credit Billing Act

3) The Fair Debt Collection Practices Act

4) The Equal Credit Opportunity Act

1) **The Fair Credit Reporting Act** summarily defines the responsibilities of creditors and credit reporting agencies when dealing with consumers. This Act also ensures the consumer's right to access his own credit file and guarantees the privacy of that information. Your basic rights as a consumer under the FCRA include:

- *Your right to access all information*—by phone, mail, or in person (except medical information) that is contained in your credit file at any consumer reporting agency.

- *Your right to have a credit reporting agency disclose* to you the nature, substance and sources of its information.

- *Your right—If you have been denied credit*, employment, or insurance because of a credit report—to know the name of the agency issuing that report.

- *Your right—If you have been denied credit within the past thirty days*, in whole or in part, as a result of a credit report issued by a credit reporting agency—to obtain a free copy of that report.

- *Your right to appear in person* to review your file.

- *Your right to dispute information* in your credit report, and to have that dispute investigated within 30 days.

- *Your right to have inaccurate or erroneous information deleted* from your credit file.

- *Your right to have the credit bureau delete* from your credit files any information that it cannot verify within 30 days.

- *Your right to have the credit bureau update* information to anyone who has received your credit file.

- *Your right to know who has been furnished a copy* of your credit report during the past six months.

- *You right to know the names of everyone* who has been furnished your credit report during the past two years.

- *Your right to include a consumer statement* in your credit report.

- *Your right to have negative credit information deleted* from your credit report after the statutory time limit for reporting such information has expired.

- *Your right to sue* a credit reporting agency.

- *Your right to be notified by anyone* requesting an investigative consumer report on you of the nature and substance of the investigation.

2) **The Fair Credit Billing Act** is specifically designed to "... protect the consumer against inaccurate and unfair credit billing and credit card practices." Your rights as a consumer under this law include:

- *Your right to challenge*, in writing, any creditor's billing statement or the amount of that billing statement.

- *Your right to have the creditor respond* within 30 days from receipt of your notice.

- *Your right to have a creditor either correct* the account or show proof that the account has been investigated and verified—within 90 days of notice.

- *Your right to have the creditor supply* you with proof that your account has been corrected or proof that your debt was verified—within 90 days of notice.

- *Your right, once you notify a creditor* that you dispute a bill, not to have your account reported as delinquent for 100 days after receiving notice from you.

- *Your right, if the account is still disputed* after the lapsed statutory time, to force the creditor to report the account "in dispute."

- *Your right to have that creditor furnish* the consumer with the name and address of every party to whom the report was furnished if an account is disputed.

- *Your right to have any settlement of the account* reported to third parties to whom reports were originally furnished.

- *Your right to have any bill* which may incur a finance charge, mailed to you at least fourteen days before the due date.

- *Your right to a refund* or credit for any overpayments.

- *Your right not be required to purchase additional* "tie-in" services in order to obtain a credit card.

3) **The Fair Debt Collection Practices Act** was enacted to protect consumers from unfair and deceptive debt collection practices. Your rights as a consumer under this law include:

- *Your right not to be abused*, harassed, or deceived by debt collectors.

- *Your right not to be contacted* by any debt collector before 8 a.m. or after 9 p.m.

- *Your right to have a debt collector* identify himself when contacting you.

- *Your right not to have a debt collector* misrepresent himself.

- *Your right—should a debt collector communicate* with a third party about you—not to have the collector mention your debt, but only seek information concerning your location. Moreover, the creditor may not communicate with any such person more than once—unless requested to do so.

- *Your right not to have a debt collector* communicate by postcard.

- *Your right not to have a debt collector* use any symbol on an envelope or telegram that indicates or refers to the debt collection business.

- *Your right—if the debt collector* has reason to believe you are represented by an attorney—not to communicate with any other person, and only communicate with you through your attorney.

- *Your right—if your employer forbids* such communication—to forbid a debt collector from communicating with you at work.

- *Your right to inform the debt collector in writing* to cease all further communication and that he must do so after informing you of any further actions to be taken.

- *Your right not to be threatened* with violence to your person or property.

- *Your right not to have your name published* as a debtor.

- *Your right not to have your debt advertised* for sale.

- *Your right not to be subject to obscene* or profane language.

- *Your right not to have a debt collector* use the telephone to harass you.

- *Your right not to have a debt collector falsely* identify himself as employed by any branch of the federal or state government.

- *Your right not to have a debt collector falsely* identify himself as an attorney.

- *Your right not to have a debt collector* falsely imply that you or your property will be subject to arrest, imprisonment, seizure, garnishment, or attachment.

- *Your right to notify the debt collector* within the statutory 30-day period, in writing, that you dispute the debt or request the name and address of the original creditor. Upon such notification, the collector must cease all debt collection activities against you pending verification of the debt. Such proof of verification must be mailed to you by the debt collector.

- *Your right to sue a debt collector* for actual and punitive damages.

4) **The Equal Credit Opportunity Act** prohibits credit discrimination on the basis of race, color, religion, national origin, sex, or marital status. You may not be denied credit because you are on public assistance or because you have exercised your rights under the Consumer Credit Protection Act. Your rights as a consumer under this law also include:

- *Your right—if you are denied credit* or have your credit revoked—to be informed by the creditor, in writing, of the specific reason for the action.

- *Your right to have the creditor supply* the information within 90 days of your written request.

- *Your right to sue* in United States District Court for both actual and punitive damages, any creditor who violates this law.

- *Your right to join in a class action suit* against the debt collector.

- *Your right to sue* under the Civil Rights Act.

Key points to remember

- Everyone needs *some* credit. Today it is unavoidable.

- We are rapidly becoming a "cashless society."

- Credit is more than necessary. It is also convenient.

- Credit is a good measure of your worth.

- Good credit represents the confidence others have in you.

- Women should establish their own independent credit apart from their husband's.

- Secured credit is backed by collateral.

- Unsecured credit is not collateralized, but is only backed by your ability and willingness to repay.

- The most common type of credit is installment credit. This may be secured or unsecured.

- Non-installment credit, whether secured or unsecured, must be repaid in a single payment by a specified date.

How Good is Your Credit?

How Good is Your Credit?

A bad credit rating is nearly impossible to hide. A vast network of credit reporting agencies track every American's credit. These bureaus are indeed the guardians of America's credit. Apply for credit at a bank or store and the prospective lender will check your credit with one or more of these credit bureaus before they issue you credit.

How America's credit reporting system works

Nearly 2,000 credit bureaus dot the United States. But only three large regional bureaus control America's credit information: Experian, TransUnion and Equifax. Experian, the largest, maintains approximately 100 million credit files, processes over 35 million credit reports each year, and services hundreds of thousands of business subscribers.

Subscribers to these major credit bureaus are the banks, lenders and nearly all businesses that give credit. Each subscriber pays a fee to obtain your credit profile, and each apparently considers it a very good investment. Subscribers know that your credit history is a good indication of your future creditworthiness. How promptly you paid past creditors reflects how you are likely to pay future creditors. Subscribers also use your credit file to verify information on your credit application.

Subscribers who receive credit information may also furnish information back to the credit bureaus. For example, when you apply for credit to a lender, that information may be forwarded to the bureau. Constant updates on your account between subscribers and the bureau keep your credit data current.

The subscribers who most commonly receive and issue credit information are the commercial banks, (including their credit card departments) other credit card companies, larger savings and loans, major department stores and finance companies.

But not all subscribers report to the credit bureaus. Others do not report their entire file. Which subscribers usually do not report? Utilities, hospitals, credit unions, oil company credit cards and bank checking and savings departments. Therefore, your bounced checks will probably not be on your credit report.

Subscribers who deal with these major credit bureaus can now easily transfer account information by periodically sending the bureau its computer disks, whether physically or through modem lines. Since the disks contain all your account information (plus changes and additions to your credit file), this ensures continuously updated credit profiles.

Profiling the three major credit bureaus

Let's take a closer look at the three major credit reporting agencies who monitor your credit on behalf of the scores of businesses you apply to for credit. The three major credit bureaus (or what the Fair Credit Reporting Act defines as "consumer reporting agencies") are:

Experian Credit Information Service (formerly TRW)
P.O. Box 2002
Allen, TX 75013-2002

TransUnion LLC
Consumer Disclosure Center
P.O. Box 1000
Chester, PA 19022-1000

EQUIFAX Credit Information Services

P.O. Box 740241

Atlanta, GA 30374-0241

Together, these three credit reporting agencies maintain files on over 200 million Americans and over 12 million businesses. Each has the ability to track the credit history of any American, regardless of where he or she may relocate. But each agency is likely to have a credit report on you, although the information will not always be the same. What appears on one credit report may not appear on another. So a thorough creditor will obtain credit reports from all three agencies to get the clearest possible picture of your credit history.

How do these agencies work? It's a relatively simple process. When you apply for credit, your creditor probably will ask a local credit bureau for your credit report. To handle this request, the creditor simply enters your name and social security number on a computer linked by modem line to the bureau. In moments, your creditor has received your complete credit profile direct from the local credit bureau.

Your local credit bureau, in turn, obtained your credit history from one of the three big reporting agencies with whom it is affiliated. Ultimately, it is the three reporting agencies that compile and disseminate your credit information. The local bureaus serve only as middlemen who disseminate the information to local creditors.

Creditors also can get credit information directly from these three national agencies, and often do. But whether creditors obtain their credit information directly or through a local credit bureau, what is important is that the computer databases of the big three agencies contain your best possible credit profile.

How your credit information is compiled

An obvious beginning question: How do the credit agencies obtain credit information about you in the first place?

Only a decade ago it was far more difficult for a credit agency to assemble your full credit picture. Now it is easily accomplished because of the computer.

Credit information about you flows through three primary sources:

1) You

2) Your creditors

3) The public records

You unintentionally provide a great deal of information about yourself whenever you apply for credit. You divulge your social security number, your job, salary, current and previous address, bank accounts, credit cards and other credit references. A detailed credit application also may disclose your assets, liabilities, alimony payments, lawsuits, judgments and prior bankruptcies.

Because you yourself provide so much of your credit information, it is critical to accurately complete your credit applications while avoiding unnecessary disclosures that would harm your credit.

Your former and current creditors also furnish information to the credit bureaus, particularly how punctually you pay your obligations. Creditors who provide the credit bureaus information may do so as either automatic subscribers or limited subscribers.

Automatic subscribers regularly supply credit information to the credit bureaus, usually on a monthly basis. Automatic subscribers report the date they first extended credit to you, your largest credit balance, the repayment terms, whether you paid punctually, and whether the bureau has pursued collection or "charged-off" your account.

Banks, credit unions, finance companies, larger merchants, collection agencies and major credit card companies (American Express, MasterCard, Visa, Discover) are ordinarily automatic subscribers.

Limited subscribers usually do not provide information to the credit bureaus. They only "buy" information. Nevertheless, a limited subscriber may report to the credit bureau your obligations. Therefore, a limited subscriber will do little to help your credit when you pay punctually, but can badly hurt your credit when you do not. As stated earlier, small banks, credit unions, hospitals, insurance companies, apartment managers and local merchants all typify limited subscribers.

Finally, information is compiled from the public records that anyone—including the credit bureaus—can access. These public records disclose lawsuits, judgments, bankruptcies, divorces, foreclosures, tax liens, wage garnishments and even criminal convictions. Private agencies search these records for adverse information and sell it to the credit bureaus.

Why you may be denied credit

Before you try to repair your credit, you must first understand why a creditor may deny you credit. The five most common reasons?

1) **Delinquent credit obligations:** Late payments, bad debts, or legal judgments against you can make you a risky customer.

2) **Incomplete credit application:** Did you forget important information or make an error on your application? Large discrepancies between your application and your credit file will hurt you as the creditor will wonder what you are hiding.

3) **Too many "inquiries":** Creditor inquiries are noted whenever you apply for credit and the creditor notifies the credit bureau. Requesting your own report also counts as an inquiry, but is usually not held against you. As few as four inquiries in six months may be considered excessive credit activity. The creditor may then presume that you are trying desperately to get credit, and are being rejected elsewhere.

4) **Errors in your file:** These may simply arise from clerical mistakes, or from confusing your name with someone with a similar name. A recent change of

address can also create problems. Since a credit bureau handles millions of files, the possibility for error is great. The only way these errors can be found and corrected is to carefully review your file for accuracy and then take the necessary steps to correct errors you do find.

5) **Insufficient credit file:** Your "credit history" is too scanty for the type or amount of credit you requested. You must then develop your credit history more fully before you qualify for the credit you are now requesting.

Always examine your credit record before applying for credit. Periodic checking is important because credit bureaus can and do make mistakes in their credit information. They may confuse you with another individual, carry erroneous information in your file, or perhaps include false, incomplete or one-sided information provided by a creditor. Most of these problems can be resolved once you understand the procedures.

Score your credit power

Score yourself. Most lenders use a scoring system to establish the credit they will extend to you. A loan officer or credit manager will disqualify you if you do not achieve a minimum number of points on the credit scoring test. The number of points required is predetermined by the creditor's policy-making committee. The loan officer or credit manager then uses it as a guide to determine whether your loan or credit request should be approved. Lending institutions chiefly utilize standardized scoring systems because it makes the process of approving loans more objective. For instance, banks know from experience that individuals at a certain salary level, say $25,000, can only handle a combined credit line of a certain amount, i.e. $2,500, on their credit cards.

Lenders also have found that people who move frequently, don't have a telephone or can't keep a steady job are also poor credit risks. Questions on the scoring test reveal these patterns. However, while the loan officer's personal judgment of the borrower is important, banks try not to rely too much on the loan officer's subjective evaluation of the borrower. By following the objective standards set by the scoring system, the banks make fewer "bad" loans.

Although each lender has its own system and asks its own questions, there are universal key questions. Know precisely what lenders look for and you can identify areas in your credit profile that you must improve to strengthen your credit-power.

THE "GOOD CREDIT" SCORING SYSTEM

Factors	Points
1. Years at present job?	
Less than one year	0
One to two years	1
Two to four years	2
Four to ten years	3
Over ten years	4
2. Monthly income level?	
Less than $1,000	0
$1,000 to $1,500	1
$1,500 to $2,000	2
Over $2,000	3
3. Present obligations past due?	
Yes	0
No	1
4. Total monthly debt payments compared to income after taxes?	
50 percent	0
40 percent to 49 percent	1
30 percent to 39 percent	2
under 30 percent	3
5. Prior loans with lender?	
No	0
Yes, but not closed	0
Yes, but closed with two or less 11-day notices	1
6. Checking account?	
None	0
Yes, but with over five rejected items in year	1
Yes, but with no rejected items over past year	2

7. Length at present address?
   Less than three years   0
   Three years or more   1

8. Age of newest automobile?
   Over one year old   0
   Less than one year old   1

9. Savings account with lender?
   No   0
   Yes   1

10. Own real estate?
   No   0
   Yes   3

11. Telephone in your own name?
   No   0
   Yes   1

12. Good credit references?
   No   0
   Yes   1

These or similar questions appear on most credit scoring systems. The questions are selected and the points are assigned by the bank's Consumer Credit Policy Committee. The policy committee then prepares guidelines for applying the scoring system to guide the loan officer. Not only will this scoring system vary between banks, but even within the same bank the criteria may change—depending on national and regional economics and the bank's local competition. Obviously, with loan money abundant, the criteria is less strictly enforced than when it is tight.

How good is your score?

Here's how a loan officer may evaluate it:

- *0 to 50 percent of possible points:* Reject outright. Don't waste time on this application.
- *50 to 60 percent of possible points:* Review very

- *50 to 60 percent of possible points:* Review very carefully. Do not approve unless there are other good reasons to grant credit.

- *60 to 70 percent of possible points:* Review with a bias toward approval. (This is the profile of the typical credit consumer and indicates a reasonable risk.)

- *70 to 90 percent of possible points:* Grant the loan unless there is good reason to deny.

- *90 to 100 percent of possible points:* Automatically grant credit within reasonable limits.

As you can see, if you fall in the lowest category, your application will be rejected outright. But don't give up. You may be able to obtain a smaller loan, or successfully pledge some collateral, or perhaps find a co-signer. (A co-signer uses his credit to guarantee your obligations.) An example may be an unemployed student who may obtain a car loan if his parents co-sign. His parent's credit would then be similarly evaluated.

If you fall between 40 percent to 90 percent then you can expect a close review of your application. Lower range applicants may require a co-signer and/or collateral. If you are above 90 percent then you can generally get any reasonable amount of unsecured credit on your signature alone.

Think about this scoring system. Obviously, each bank keeps its point system secret, and only the loan officer knows how many points you need to pass the credit test. But you can improve your chances for winning credit by knowing the system.

Later chapters will show you how to build more powerful credit. But for now, don't forget those other negative marks on your credit rating that can destroy your chances for credit:

1) Too many delinquent accounts, "slow pay" or "no pay" or accounts turned over for collection or "charged off." (The creditor has stopped pursuing collection and does not expect repayment).

2) Unsatisfied judgments or tax liens.

4) Foreclosure or repossession.

These are the "credit killers" on your credit report that you must erase if you are to get the credit you want.

What your credit report discloses

Credit reports vary slightly between agencies. However, most credit reports include:

1) **Identification information:** your full name, last two addresses, social security number, date of birth, and place of employment, if known. Length of employment and income are typically not reported, but if reported, often are incorrect. Creditors may reject credit applications when they cannot confirm employment. Are you self-employed? The credit bureau may incorrectly list you as unemployed, and this too should be corrected immediately.

2) **Detailed information on the listed accounts:** name of the issuer, date account was opened, original balance or limit, current balance (beginning with the reporting date, which is also listed), terms of account, and the current status of the account. The status of each item follows a complicated coding system that details the account history. This is why there is no opportunity to pay a delinquent account and change your status to "cleared." An example is CO NOW PAY, which means that the account was a "charge-off," but that you are now paying on the account.

3) **Public record information:** Bankruptcies, tax liens, judgments, foreclosures, divorces and other public filings.

4) **Credit report requests:** whenever someone requests a copy of your report it is recorded in your report and remains on your record for up to one year. This addition is "non-evaluated" by the bureau, but it can be a "negative" if you have too many inquiries with comparatively few opened accounts. Prospective

creditors then question why you were turned down although there are many possible reasons for the inquiries.

5) **Consumer statement:** Finally, your report has a space for you to place a consumer statement. Here you may challenge or explain any creditor entry in your file with a 100-word or less statement.

What your credit report cannot disclose

Your credit report cannot contain information concerning your race, religion, sex or personal lifestyle. Your credit report also cannot contain information concerning your character.

A credit application may request the names and addresses of relatives or associates. However the credit bureaus may not solicit them for credit information, but may only contact them to verify residence, employment or to locate you should you default in payment.

Do not confuse a credit report with another report called an Investigative Consumer Report. This is not part of the credit system and is prepared by companies who specialize in compiling detailed profiles on individuals. These reports contain considerably more personal information than is found in a credit report. The Federal Fair Credit Reporting Act requires that you be notified if an Investigative Consumer Report is prepared on you.

Your credit report also will not reflect your entire credit history. Many creditors are limited subscribers to the credit bureaus and won't release credit information to the credit bureaus. Other creditors may have no affiliation with a credit bureau. Therefore, only a small percentage of your credit transactions may actually appear on your credit report. What is important is that those few transactions be accurate and favorable.

How to get your credit report

Not everyone can obtain your credit report. Section 1681b of the Fair Credit Reporting Act provides that only businesses and individuals with a legitimate business need for the information in connection with a business transaction that involves you may do so. This goes beyond creditors to whom you have applied for credit, such as credit card issuers, lenders, and businesses with whom you want charge privileges. It would, for example, also extend to a court order or a subpoena issued in connection with a Federal grand jury inquiry, insurance companies underwriting insurance for the consumer, or any government agency that must consider the consumer's financial responsibility in connection with the issuing of a license, or a prospective employer.

A prospective employer—or anyone requesting a credit report that contains medical information—must get your permission before they can have access to your file, and all of the above mentioned parties may access your credit files only for credit-related purposes. It would be a violation of federal law for someone without a legitimate credit-related purpose to access your files.

The Fair Credit Reporting Act guarantees you access to your own credit report, or at least the basic information that is sent to creditors. Specifically, the credit bureau must disclose:

1) The nature and substance of all information (except for medical information) on file at the time of your request.

2) The sources of information concerning you.

3) The name of any party who received your credit report for employment purposes within the prior two years.

4) The name of any party who has received your credit report for any other purpose within the prior six months.

If a creditor has not denied you credit within the prior 30 days the credit bureau may charge you a "reasonable charge" for a copy of your credit report. The fees vary between bureaus and even different regional offices of the same agency. Therefore, you should check with the credit bureau before you formally request your credit report. Generally, the fees are under $10.

If you have been refused credit within 30 days based on a credit report from the credit bureau from whom you now seek a report, then the credit report is free. The bureaus must honor a request for a free report anytime within 60 days after credit is refused. Keep in mind that credit bureaus that did not issue a report on which credit was denied can still charge you a credit report fee. You are entitled to only one free report each year per bureau.

It is not difficult to obtain your credit report. The most common method is to write directly to the agency. (See sample letter number 1A). Your letter should state:

1) Your full name (and any aliases or maiden name)

2) Current address

3) Former address

4) Social security number

5) Spouse's name (this is voluntary)

6) Whether you have been denied credit within 30 days (include a copy of the credit denial or the details related thereto)

Each bureau may require additional information (such as a photocopy of your driver's license), so it is recommended that you first contact the bureau from which you are requesting a report.

You may also visit the credit bureau in person. The bureau will then require you to complete a credit report request form that contains the above information.

It is not difficult to contact the credit bureaus. You will know who to contact if you have been denied credit because the creditor must then send you a letter explaining why you were denied credit and the credit information source.

You can contact the big three credit bureaus at the following addresses:

Experian Credit Information Service (formerly TRW)

P.O. Box 2002

Allen, TX 75013-2002

www.experian.com

TransUnion LLC

Consumer Disclosure Center

P.O. Box 1000

Chester, PA 19022-1000

www.transunion.com

EQUIFAX Credit Information Services

P.O. Box 740241

Atlanta, GA 30374-0241

www.equifax.com

How to read and evaluate your credit report

Once you have your credit report, you must know how to identify credit problems.

First, find and circle each of the negative remarks or "dings" in your credit file. Information on these reports is usually coded like your bank statement. To assist you, the FCRA requires credit bureaus to explain anything on the report that you cannot reasonably understand. So, you will find a key to the coding symbols. Next look for damaging remarks in these four sections of your report:

- **The Historical Status** records of your monthly payments. Ideally, this should be free of "past due" symbols which may be 30, 60 or 90-day periods. Many of the bad marks can be "past due" symbols which could be entered accidentally or because the mail with your payment was late, or because of delays in processing your payments. Of course, you also may have actually made late payments. Remember that to avoid late payment marks you must have your payments credited to your accounts before the due date, not just mailed by that time.

- **The Comments** section may, for instance, contain remarks such as "charged to P&L." "P&L" means "profit and loss." When a creditor charges an account to profit and loss, that means it has charged it off as a bad debt loss and that it does not expect to be able to collect. Other negative entries may include:

    COLL ACCT. Your account has been assigned to a collection agency because it is seriously past due.

    CURR WAS FOR. Foreclosure proceedings were started on your account but you repaid all past due amounts and the account is now current.

    CURR WAS 30-2. Twice your account has been 30 days past due but is now current.

    DEED IN LIEU. In order to prevent a creditor from foreclosing, you gave him or her a deed to your property.

    DEL WAS 120. Your account was 120 days past due. Although you made some payments, your account is still 30, 60, or 90 days late.

    GOVCLAIM. The government filed a claim against you because you failed to repay a government loan.

    FORECLOSURE. Your creditor foreclosed on your property.

    NOT PAY AA. You still have an outstanding balance and are not paying according to the agreement.

    REPO. Your creditor repossessed your property because you failed to repay your loan.

    VOL SURR. You voluntarily surrendered your property to prevent repossession by a creditor.

    30 DAY DEL. You are at least 30 days late on one or more payments on your account.

Any of these marks, of course, signifies a bad credit risk.

Inquiries made by banks, stores or others from whom you applied for credit will also be listed in the report. "Too many" inquiries may be taken by a potential creditor as an indication that you are in financial difficulty and may be seeking more credit as a solution. Creditors often refuse to give credit on the basis of "too many" inquiries. How many inquiries are "too many" is subjective. However, as few as four or five in six months may be excessive for some creditors.

Public record data can appear in your credit report and these entries must also be examined closely for accuracy.

- **Bankruptcy**—by filing for bankruptcy you admitted that you once were financially unable to pay your debts when due.
- **Tax Lien**—an IRS or state tax lien was entered against your property because you owe taxes.
- **Judgment**-you lost a lawsuit either at trial or because you failed to defend, and there is now a judgment on record against you.
- **Settled**—before trial you resolved a pending lawsuit.
- **Child Support**—you failed to pay court-ordered child support.
- **Withdrawn**—your bankruptcy case was withdrawn.
- **Dismissed**—your case was dismissed because either the court ruled in your favor or the creditor failed to show up.
- **Discharged**—you filed bankruptcy and the court relieved you of your debts.
- **Paid and Satisfied**—you fully paid a court judgement or an account submitted for collection.
- **Suit**—a legal action is pending against you.

Finally, your credit report will include a column with a title such as "Account Profile." This column contains a summary rating for each account. A summary may read "positive," "negative" or "non-rated." "Positive means you pay on time. "Negative" means you have a serious credit problem, perhaps a defaulted debt. "Non-rated" may signify a few late payments among many prompt payments, which still gives you a weak credit even when there is no strongly negative entry. Each negative or non-rated entry has a code that reflects the nature of the problem. Your goal: To protest and eventually remove every negative or non-rated profile.

Your personal information is another potentially troublesome section to check carefully. Bureaus often employ "alert codes" to highlight conflicting information in your file. Such terms as "HAWK ALERT, TransAlert, AKA search, or CHECKPOINT" on your credit report imply that you may have tried to alter your file, although conflicting information may have resulted instead from a processing or typing error. Remember, even one incorrect digit in your social security number could make it appear that you are trying to defraud creditors.

The alert can also mean that the credit bureau received four or more inquiries about your report within the last 60 days. The credit bureau is then warning creditors that you may have a sudden need for credit or, for instance, the alert may also indicate that the credit bureau believes that your residential address is really a commercial address. Whatever the warning, the alert makes it seem as though you are trying to deceive the credit bureau and its subscribers.

Some credit bureaus now use a new index called a "delinquency indicator" which is supposed to more accurately predict whether you will promptly pay your debts. Unfortunately, credit bureaus are required neither to disclose the components of this index nor explain how to read it. Consequently, you cannot dispute the accuracy of this index.

Credit Scoring

The three large credit bureaus have each adopted a ranking or scoring system called a credit score or FICO® score, by which, for a fee, you can receive a numerical evaluation of your present credit condition. This is meant to approximate the score you would receive from a lender such as a bank. The credit score is compiled directly from the positive and negative factors found in your credit report. The score is divided into five categories and breaks down as follows:

Type of credit you use =10%

Your credit history =35%

Amount currently owed =30%

Length of your credit history =15%

New credit obtained =10%

Equifax uses a scoring system which ranges between 300 and 850, TransUnion's system ranges between 150 and 934 and Experian's system ranges from 340 to 820.

For example, under the Experian scoring system a score of

340-600 = highest possible risk to the lender

601-660 = medium-high risk

661-720 = medium risk

721-780 = medium-low risk

781-820 = low risk

When you receive your numerical credit score, you will also receive a national percentile ranking. This number reflects the percentage of the US population with scores higher or lower than yours. For example, under the Experian system, a credit score of 800 puts you into the 92 percentile. This means that only 8% of the population had higher scores than you while 92% of the population had lower scores than you.

Higher scores mean lower delinquency rates. This is the rate at which 100 borrowers in a specific range will default on a loan, declare bankruptcy, or fall 90 days behind in their payments. Thus, a delinquency rate of 50% means that out of 100 borrowers 50 will commit one of the above.

Common factors that can lower your score include:

- *Owning too many credit cards*—simply owning too many credit cards increases your potential for indebtedness.

- *Too many current accounts with outstanding balances*—regardless of your ability to pay, lenders view this as a potential problem.

- *Failure to significantly reduce loan amounts*—your level of debt is too high in relation to your total credit limit and to your total loan amounts. The best strategy is to have few debts and keep balances low.

Be aware that while a lender will certainly evaluate your credit history, it is only one component of the final decision. Your income, employment history, assets, liabilities, and numerous other factors play a significant role in his decision to offer credit. While there are many different scoring models, and not all bureaus use the same model, lenders will use the score as a timesaving summary of your credit report.

Some credit bureaus charge for the score, some provide it for free if you purchase your credit report, and others tie the score to a subscription package.

Since your credit score is based upon your credit report, the way to improve your credit score is by improving your credit report.

Remember, credit bureaus accept without your knowledge any negative information about you whether from a creditor or other source, and regardless of whether it is true. The credit bureau is under no obligation to check the accuracy of this credit information until you challenge it. Unfortunately, creditors will rely heavily upon the information in your credit report—though the credit bureau has no responsibility for its accuracy. The burden is on you to keep your report as accurate as possible.

Key points to remember

- The three major credit bureaus, Experian, Trans Union, and Equifax are collectively responsible for over 200 million credit files.

- Utilities, hospitals, credit unions, oil company credit cards, and bank checking and savings departments do not usually report accounts to the credit bureaus.

- The Fair Credit Reporting Act was designed to protect consumers from unfair credit reporting practices.

- Learn how to read your credit report by studying the explanatory codes.

- Always check your credit report for accuracy.

- Remember, only someone with a legitimate credit-related purpose may have access to your credit report.

- The Fair Credit Reporting Act guarantees you access to your own file.

- If you have been refused credit within 30 days based on a credit report from the bureau from whom you seek a report, the report is free. Otherwise, expect a nominal charge.

- Obtain a copy of your credit report, identify the negative entries or "dings," and begin the process of clearing your credit following the strategies in the next chapter.

How To Repair Your Credit

3

How To Repair Your Credit

Before you can demand your legal rights, you must thoroughly know your legal rights. These are contained in the four sections of the Consumer Protection Act. The Fair Credit Reporting Act section (FCRA), is primarily concerned with credit bureaus and credit reports. The intent of the FCRA is twofold: 1) To protect you against credit abuses and 2) To provide you with the legal tools to repair and improve your credit.

What can you do if your credit report contains false, misleading or incomplete information that now injures your credit?

To begin, you must turn to the Fair Credit Reporting Act (FCRA) which protects you against credit abuse that might result from an unfair profile of your creditworthiness. It does this by granting you five important rights as a credit consumer. Take advantage of these five basic rights. They are your key to erasing those negative marks in your credit report and to regaining good credit.

Enforce your legal rights for good credit

Right No. 1:   You can challenge the accuracy of your credit report at any time. Your right to challenge your report is found in section 1681i of the FCRA under "Procedure in case of disputed accuracy." By "disputed accuracy " the law refers to any information in your report that is false, obsolete, incomplete or incorrectly entered, in whole or in part.

Section 1681c, clearly defines the length of time negative information can remain on your credit report. Older information is considered obsolete and must by law, be removed. For example, the law allows a bankruptcy or an unpaid IRS tax lien to remain on your report for 10 years. Most other information is considered obsolete after 7 years.

Bear in mind, that when you dispute an entry, you neither admit nor deny your liability for the debt. You are simply challenging the *accuracy* of what is reported on your credit statement.

Right No. 2: The credit bureau must "reinvestigate" whatever you challenge. Section 1681i of the FCRA also forces the credit bureau to contact the creditor and request that the creditor verify the information exactly as it appears on your report. Remember, any person or company—whether a legitimate creditor or not—can enter negative information on your credit report without your consent or knowledge—and without the need to first prove it is true. Since the credit bureaus are only considered reporting agencies, they too need not prove the accuracy of the information—unless you challenge it!

Right No. 3: The credit bureau must reinvestigate within 30 days. Credit bureaus have 30 days to reinvestigate any disputed item on your report.The exception to this is a 15 day extension should the consumer offer additional information relevant to the disputed item. This procedure also is outlined in FCRA section 1681i.

Right No. 4: If the bureau cannot confirm the adverse information against you, it must promptly delete that erroneous information from its files. This puts the burden of proof back on the original creditor. And make no mistake, it is burdensome. The information needed for a creditor to verify is rarely easily accessed. The original creditor may need to locate and search through old files. The information must then be thoroughly checked for accuracy and completeness. And the creditor must then respond to the credit bureau within the statutory time period presenting legal proof of its claim against you. In fact, this is simply *too* burdensome a task for most creditors to complete within the required time. This means you can probably delete most negative remarks against you through creditor default.

Right No. 5: **If the original creditor verifies the information and the bureau responds timely, the negative marks must remain on your record.** But if you still dispute the information reported you have the right to submit a Consumer Statement of your view of the problem. In other words, if you as a credit consumer, dispute the accuracy of information on your report, and you receive no satisfaction from the bureau or the creditor, then the credit bureau must attach your explanation (not to exceed 100 words) to every copy of your credit report it later issues.

Seven key steps to repair your credit

With this understanding of your legal rights, and with your credit report in hand, you are now ready to repair your credit following this proven seven-step credit repair plan:

Step 1. **Find and circle each of the negative marks or "dings" on your credit report.** The information on your credit report will be coded like your bank statement. However, the FCRA requires credit bureaus to explain any item on their report that you cannot reasonably understand without a key to their coding.

Damaging credit remarks can be found in several sections of your report. The Historical Status records your monthly payments. Ideally, this will be free of "past due" symbols which may be 30, 60 or 90 day periods. Most bad marks are "past dues." List each "past due" account on a separate sheet of paper. How many past dues do you have? How late were these payments? What percentage of your total accounts fall within the delinquent category? You will see how to contest these negatives or "dings" in Step 3.

Some "past dues" may be entered accidentally, or because the mail containing your payment was delivered late, or because of a delay in processing your payment. Of course, you may also have paid late. You must have your payment actually credited to your account before the due date, not merely mailed by that date—if you are to avoid a late payment mark.

The Comments section may contain remarks such as "Charged to P&L." "P&L" means "profit and loss." When a company charges an account to profit and loss, it has charged it off as a bad debt and no longer expects to collect, which, of course, indicates a bad credit risk.

Credit inquiries from banks, stores, credit card companies or others to whom you applied for credit will also be listed in your report. Too many credit inquiries may be seen by a potential creditor as an indication that you are in financial difficulty and are seeking more credit as a solution. Creditors refuse credit when there are too many inquiries. How many is "too many?" This is for each creditor to decide. To counteract "too many inquiries" use a 100-word (or less) statement added to your credit report to explain in a positive way why you have so many credit inquiries.

Public records information will also appear in your credit report including tax liens, bankruptcies, or court judgments against you. Closely examine these entries for accuracy. How can you put these in a more favorable light?

Step 2. Determine your overall credit score. Your credit report will have a column with a title such as "Account Profile" which contains a summary rating for each of your accounts. A summary may read "positive," "negative" or "non-rated." "Positive" means good credit. You pay on time. "Negative" means serious credit problems. Perhaps you have defaulted on a major debt or filed bankruptcy. "Non-rated" means a few late payments. This, however, still weakens your credit. Each negative or non-rated entry has a code reflecting the nature of the problem. Your goal is to protest and remove all negative or non-rated profiles.

Step 3.   Protest each "ding" to the credit bureau. To exercise your legal rights, you must aggressively challenge any bad marks. The credit bureau need only verify the facts if you assert that they are in error. So stand up for your rights! Send a strong but polite protest for each item you want to challenge and tell the credit bureau you are exercising your rights under the FCRA.

For example, if you find the code "Charge Off," the creditor charged your account to profit and loss, and the creditor thinks your debt is uncollectible. You could protest that this comment should be removed *if* the debt was satisfied. Therefore, it should not be reported as a charge off. Or there may be a series of Past Dues. Perhaps those payments were delayed due to a mix-up with the post office when you changed addresses.

You may also dispute owing the creditor the amount claimed as delinquent or charged off. Were you billed for unsatisfactory goods or services? Did the creditor fail to resolve the problem to your satisfaction? Was there a delay in rectifying the problem that explains your delay in payment? You see the many possible reasons you may have for disputing a negative credit mark.

Send a protest letter only if you believe the negative credit mark should not be entered against you because it was due to problems with the creditor, is factually incorrect or misleading or was due to circumstances beyond your control. If the negative information is factually correct but there are extenuating or mitigating circumstances for the negative entry, then this is best handled with a 100-word statement added to your credit report.

With the sample letters at the end of this book as your guide, write your letter of dispute to the credit bureau. Never use the dispute form supplied by the credit bureau because their dispute forms are carefully designed to limit you to a specific reason for your dispute. The law, however, requires only that you give a general reason.

Next, carefully list each ding that you want to challenge and then draft your protest. List all the items that you want to dispute in your first letter. Do not write separate letters for each item. If you try to dispute one entry at a time, the credit bureau will consider your requests as "frivolous and irrelevant" and will then be able to legally ignore your request for an investigation.

Remember, *offer only general reasons* for your dispute. *Avoid specific reasons*, such as incorrect dollar amounts or dates. For example, suppose the credit bureau inaccurately reports that you owe $1,500 when you owe $1,475. Your dispute should only state that you never owed that creditor $1,500. You are not obligated to say what you do owe, nor should you mention it. Or for a disputed date, simply claim that you never incurred that debt on *that* date. Say no more. Or if you fully paid the debt, say so, but don't say when. Do not give the credit bureau more negative information to add to your report. Make the credit bureau do their own work!

Step 4. Put it in writing. Never send a form or pre-printed letter to the credit bureau. When you use the sample letters in this book, write them by hand or re-type them on plain paper with no letterhead. The reason is that you do not want it to appear that your letter originated from a credit repair company or an attorney because these are either automatically returned or sent to their legal department. A handwritten letter starts the process sooner. Also be sure your letter is signed, dated, and includes your address, date of birth and social security number. Copy your letter for your records. Send your letters certified mail, return receipt requested. You can then prove when the bureau received it. Finally, include a copy of your credit report to ensure the bureau checks the right file.

If for some reason you cannot send the credit bureau a hand written letter, then retype the sample letters provided in this book so that they do not appear as form letters. But do change them slightly so they do not precisely match other letters that they receive.

Keep *everything* in writing! Never waste time communicating with a credit bureau either by telephone or in person. Credit repair strategy requires everything to be in writing. Moreover, your communication must state certain information, which is why you must closely follow the sample letters in this book.

Also log your written communication. You particularly want to track when correspondence was received by the credit bureau and when a reply is required.

Step 5. Wait for the credit bureau to reply. The credit bureau must respond to your initial letter within 30 days as outlined in FCRA section 1681i.

If the credit bureau does not reply within 30 days, then send a second letter demanding an immediate response to your request.

The credit bureau should ultimately respond in one of three ways:

Alternative #1

The credit bureau corrects the mistakes.

This, of course, is the response you want because it corrects the errors in your credit report; errors that are causing you bad credit. This may occur in one of two ways.

1) *The creditor agrees to the correction.* Upon receiving your letter, the credit bureau will notify the creditor of the dispute and request that the creditor "verify" the negative credit entry. If the creditor agrees that you are correct and that the negative entry is the result of a mistake, then the creditor may notify the credit bureau to clear your credit record.

2) *The creditor did not verify the negative credit mark.* In most instances the creditor will not reply to the credit bureau and the negative credit mark against you will remain unverified. Since the negative credit mark that you had challenged was not verified, the credit bureau must remove the disputed item from your credit report.

This, of course, is how 90 percent of all negative credit marks are deleted from credit reports and how credit is usually repaired. So let's repeat the steps:

- You dispute the credit entry.
- The credit bureau requests verification from the creditor.
- The creditor fails to verify the adverse credit information.
- The credit bureau is now required to reply to you within 30 days and must report that since the disputed credit entry was not verified by the creditor, it will be deleted.

Remember, a credit bureau cannot on its own verify credit information. It *must* rely on the creditor to defend against your dispute. Only in this way can the negative mark be verified and allowed to remain on your credit report.

Why wouldn't a creditor defend against your dispute and verify the negative credit information that he himself provided the credit bureau? There may be several reasons. As stated, the most common is that the creditor simply didn't want to be bothered. Creditors are for the most part busy businesspeople. While it is comparatively easy for them to initially report a credit problem to a credit bureau, verification months or years later is considerably more difficult. The creditor, at the least, will have to locate your file, provide supporting documents and furnish a detailed statement as part of the verification process. Most creditors find it easier to simply ignore the request for verification. This clears your credit.

And this is precisely how expensive credit repair firms clear their client's credit. And if it seems that you are taking unfair advantage of a procedural loophole to repair your credit, you must keep in mind that both the Federal Trade Commission and Congress want it that way. They believe that the burden should be on the creditor to defend any adverse credit marks filed against you. And if the creditor cannot, or chooses not to, then you the consumer should not be penalized by that unverified credit mark!

Alternative #2

The credit bureau verifies the disputed item is correct and thus keeps it on your credit record.

Some creditors will verify the negative mark. In this instance, the credit bureau should confirm this to you within the 30-day reply period. The credit bureau's reply to you will contain the creditor's statement and/or documentation to verify the negative credit information. Should this occur, the credit bureau probably will not change your credit report and the negative credit mark will remain on your credit report.

This does not mean there is nothing further you can do to correct your credit report. You then have three key options:

1) Wait and try again. Wait a year or two and again challenge the negative item, but then raise a different dispute. If the creditor once verified the disputed item, it would be frivolous to file the same dispute a second time. However, if you can raise a new dispute, it may be worth the effort. Again, the creditor may either agree with you, fail to defend, or "verify" the negative mark.

2) Convince the credit bureau that you are correct. It is not the role of the credit bureau to referee whether you or your creditor is correct on a disputed credit entry. If the creditor provides reasonably sufficient information to verify or defend its negative credit entry against you, the credit bureau may keep the negative mark on your record. But it need not! The credit bureau does not act as an arbiter or a court to determine whether you or your creditor is correct. However, a credit bureau does have the responsibility to act fairly and use reasonable care to make certain that it reports only truthful, accurate information. So the credit bureau can correct information on your report if you can convince the credit bureau that the negative entry against you is erroneous.

Build your case! Send the credit bureau a clear statement that explains why the information is erroneous. Submit all documents (canceled checks, letters) that corroborate your claim.

Perhaps you sent this detailed information when you first disputed your credit report. If the creditor defended his negative entry, you can only send a second letter that challenges more specific points made by the creditor. Most often, the first letter only summarily challenges the negative mark with a brief explanation. Of course, if the creditor does not verify the reasons for the negative mark, the mark must be removed. It is usually when the creditor verifies that you must build a stronger case to convince the credit bureau that you, not your creditor, are correct.

If the credit bureau still refuses to change your credit report, then your one remaining option is to talk to the creditor directly.

Most creditors are reasonable and will listen to any claim that they may have made an error or in some way unfairly penalized you with poor credit. Persuade your creditor that your claim is legitimate and the creditor can have the credit bureau correct your credit report. This commonly occurs.

Alternative #3

The credit bureau only sends you a preliminary response.

Your first reply from the credit bureau may be a preliminary letter that acknowledges receipt of your protest letter, but merely advises you that the bureau has not concluded its investigation.

Credit bureaus frequently send a preliminary response to request additional information. It may be canceled checks or perhaps evidence that a tax lien or judgment has been satisfied. You, of course, should fully and quickly comply with the request. Also inquire when you can expect the investigation to be completed, and a final determination made, and of course, when your credit report will be changed.

Caution: Credit bureaus do stall

- The credit bureau may ask you to verify your identity. Send them a copy of a bill that reveals as little about you as possible. A current phone or utility bill or some other bill with account information they are already likely to have in their computer will do. Never send a copy of your driver's license, social security card or identification that reveals your place of employment.

- The credit bureau may claim you are using a credit repair company, and thus, refuse to investigate. Respond with sample letter #12 in this book. It is specifically designed for this problem.

- The credit bureau may claim your dispute is "frivolous and irrelevant" and ignore your request. Sample letter #11 is specifically designed for this problem.

If the credit bureau does not send you a final reply within 30 days (or such other reasonable time that they may specify), then the negative credit information against you *must* be removed. If the credit bureau does not change your credit report, then you must proceed as under the previous section.

Step 6. Request your updated credit report. Once you complete your credit repair process, request an updated copy of your credit report. The FCRA requires the credit bureau to send a free credit report update to anyone who has received a copy of the report within six months previous to any corrections or statements that are added to their credit reports. They will also send a free credit report update to anyone who requested your credit report for employment purposes within the prior two years. You also are entitled to a free update. But you must request it to receive it. So be sure to make your request, and also request the bureau to send an update to anyone you know who has recently inquired about your credit. While the credit bureau is not required to send a copy of the entire report, it often will because that is more convenient to them.

Do not send updated reports to creditors until all the possible corrections to your credit report have been made. Only then will you be able to present to a prospective creditor the best possible credit report.

Compare carefully your updated credit report with the original. Mark every change or improvement that you find. Circle every negative that has moved up to non-rated as well as any non-rated or negatives that became positive. You will probably not get results on every protest on the first round, but with perseverance some progress is likely. You will notice that the bureau has probably deleted some negative items only because one or more creditors failed to punctually respond to the investigation. This too is more common than you would believe!

Step 7. Repeat the process. Do you still have negative marks? Start over! Repeat this process at least twice before moving on to the next phase. Bad credit cannot be repaired in a day. It takes patience and persistence. But you should have fewer negative items to dispute on the second round. A creditor who responded promptly the first time, may be less diligent the second or third time. Also remember that during this process you must not allow any new credit problems to appear on your credit record. Keep all your accounts current—even pay ahead of schedule!

Seven more little-known credit repair strategies

Here are seven additional techniques to try after you twice used the process and still have several stubborn marks on your credit report.

1. Send your second dispute letter to a different branch office of the same credit bureau. This tactic is very effective if you once lived in another part of the country. You will have to justify this transfer of your file to the new office, but this is easy. Simply state in your letter that since you once lived in that area, some of the disputes originated there.

2. Send your second dispute letter to the "Vice President of Customer Relations," at the main headquarters of the credit bureau. This individual has the power to begin his or her own investigation—from the top down!

3. Try to establish a personal or friendly relationship with someone at the credit bureau. If you receive something signed by someone at the bureau, send your subsequent letters to the attention of that person.

4. Send your requests to the legal department of the credit bureau. This is an especially effective tactic if you dispute obsolete entries which must legally be removed.

5. Challenge all information reported as "confirmed" by the credit bureau. Section 609a(2) of the FCRA states "Every consumer reporting agency shall, upon request and proper identification of any consumer, clearly and accurately disclose to the consumer . . . [t]he sources of the information." This means you have the right to ask for:

    a. The name, address, and phone numbers of those creditors who supposedly verified the information. If there is an intermediary such as a collection agency, this will require additional time because the collection agency must contact the original creditor. But collection agencies are notoriously reluctant to do so because this earns them no money. Likewise, the original creditor must waste time and money to gather the information and send it to the collection agency.

    b. An explanation of how the information was verified. Verification by phoning the collection agency without contacting the original creditor is not sufficient proof of a debt.

    c. Proof that the information was legally verified. The credit bureau must be able to offer you proof that they first attempted to contact the original creditor. This is important ammunition because the credit bureau may not have attempted verification but simply sent your original report back to you unchanged.

6. File a formal dispute with the Sub-Committee on Banking, Credit and Insurance. Unlike the Federal Trade Commission, this committee is interested in individual issues and problems in the credit reporting field. Send them copies of your credit reports, all written communication between yourself and the credit

bureau, and an explanation of your problems. Send the information to:

> Subcommittee on Banking, Credit, and Insurance
> 604 O'Neil House Building
> Washington, DC 20515
> (202) 225-8872

7. Domino one cleared report into two more. If you are fortunate to have received at least one credit report completely cleared, send copies of the proofs that the negative entries were deleted to the other credit bureaus that had the same negative marks, and request that they remove the negative accounts from their credit report. *Before you attempt this, make absolutely sure that there is nothing negative on your credit report that can hurt you if disclosed to the other credit bureaus.*

Gain your creditor's cooperation

Negative entries cannot always be deleted without creditor cooperation because the entries are accurate and the creditor persistently cooperates with the bureau's request for verification. Your goal then is to persuade the creditor to either tone down or entirely delete his remarks on your credit report. Later, we will deal with the bad debts that you still owe and where you must be even more persuasive with your creditors, but for now, we only want to turn those late payment marks into positive credit ratings. Follow these five simple steps :

Step 1. Set up a worksheet for each creditor

Accurate recordkeeping is essential when dealing with creditors who insist upon defending their bad marks. Create a creditor worksheet with the name, account numbers, credit remarks, and any documents, correspondence or notes you have concerning the creditor.

Step 2. Write to each creditor

After studying the facts concerning each account and the nature of the credit complaint, write the creditor explaining your version of how the problem arose. Be specific. Submit relevant details and full documentation. Be factual, but also appeal to the creditor's sense of goodwill. Perhaps your company went bankrupt suddenly or you lost your job. Or perhaps you were detained several weeks in a foreign country while on a business trip and therefore unable to pay your accounts on time. Remind the creditor that you eventually paid and that you appreciated his services and products in spite of your payment problems. Appeal to the creditor's compassion and ask him to either remove the bad marks now that the account is settled, or at least put in a statement that the account is paid.

As you write the letter, consider it in light of other accounts that may have been affected by the same circumstances. Each letter you send should be consistent with the others so if the creditor's new comments do appear on your credit file they will appear reasonable and consistent. Forget lame excuses for poor bill-paying habits. Use strong, compelling reasons. Send your letter by certified mail, return receipt requested, and keep a copy of each letter and receipt with your worksheet file.

Frequently your creditor won't back down. However, you may still question the accuracy or completeness of the entry the creditor has filed against you. As you will see later, it is your right to add to your credit file your version of the situation. Your comments to why the bill was not timely paid must be submitted under any credit request. Your comments may greatly mitigate the damage of a particular entry.

You may not want to comment on any one particular entry, but instead have your credit record reflect reasons for a generally poor credit. For example, if you have several negative entries, were they caused by:

• A layoff from work?
• Divorce?

- Personal or family illness?
- Tax problems?

You see the idea. These unfortunate situations can hit anyone and wreak havoc on an otherwise excellent credit history. Let credit inquirers know if there was one definable event that ruined your good credit. Point out your prior track record. Convince creditors that these problems are behind you and unlikely to recur.

Step 3. Order an updated credit report after 30 days

Quite often creditors will cooperate and remove negative marks. Allow about 30 days for the creditor to respond to your letter and then order a new credit report to see if the creditor changed your report. Have the remaining bad marks been deleted? Have softer remarks been substituted or added?

Now the ball is again with the credit bureau. Wait the estimated time that you established during your first campaign when you initially tried to persuade the bureau to remove the negative marks. The bureau should reply within a few weeks with an updated copy of your report.

Step 4. Telephone the creditor

If letters prove futile, try the telephone. The telephone is a more personal way to interact with the creditor. But before you call, study the credit report information, your creditor's responses and the worksheet you have compiled. Next outline each point you wish to make during your call.

Step 5. Be persistent

The first call to a creditor may have no effect. Don't be bashful or discouraged. Try again. Be persistent. Talk to a different person. Large companies have many people in their credit and customer relations departments and each will react differently to you. You may eventually find someone who will cooperate. Once a creditor agrees that a change in your report is justified, have the creditor verbally agree to change your credit status. Follow with a letter confirming that agreement. Have the creditor sign the letter and return it to you for your own records. This letter is important because if the creditor forgets or later refuses to change your status, you can then send the letter to the credit bureau.

Turn today's financial problems into a positive credit rating

You can successfully turn even current bad debts into a positive credit rating. How? Approach your creditors and negotiate repayment plans that sincerely demonstrate your ability to make regular payments to fully pay your debts and revive their interest in you as a customer. In return? Your creditors will restore your positive credit rating.

Here's the six-point strategy:

1. *If your account is with a collection agency.* If your account has already been sent to a collection agency, then deal first with the creditor. A collection agency receives a percentage of what they collect from you so they only care to collect as much as they can from you. The creditor, on the other hand, may not expect full payment. And your future business may also be important. When you deal with the creditor you usually have more flexibility to negotiate time or amount of payment. However, creditors frequently refuse to deal with customers after an account has been turned over to an attorney or collection agency. Because the collection agency is not consumer oriented and is usually more difficult to negotiate with, avoid having the debt turned over for collection. If you cannot avoid negotiating with the collection agency, the following points for effectively dealing with the creditor can be as successfully used with the collection agency.

2. *Make a win-win offer to the creditor.* Your goal here is to trade some money for a positive credit rating. Perhaps you can set up a payment schedule in exchange for a corrected credit entry. For example, agree to pay what

you owe in 12 monthly installments if the creditor agrees to reward you with an improved credit rating. Be specific. Or agree that after three months of punctual payments, your negative rating will be raised to a non-rating, and after six months the non-rating lifted to a positive rating. You see the idea!

3. *Obtain open account status.* It won't help if your account is closed for further purchases while you now make regular payments. So when negotiating, ask your creditor to reopen your account while you uphold your end of the agreement. You are more persuasive if you offer to fully pay the debt with interest or an added service charge. Be certain that whatever terms you finally agree upon are within your budget so you faithfully keep your promise.

4. *Put it in writing.* Win-win negotiations can begin by telephone, but do reduce your verbal agreement to writing. Carefully list each point of agreement and recite them over the phone for the creditor's verification. Follow with a letter to the creditor with a stamped, self-addressed envelope. However, you may want your lawyer to check the agreement. Once the creditor signs and returns the agreement and returns it to you, it can become part of your credit record.

5. *Honor the agreement.* Now that you have a written agreement, you need only fulfill it for your credit rating to be restored. So be punctual. Make every payment on time. Be responsible. If your ability to pay should, for example, be threatened by unemployment or illness, then inform your creditor *before* you miss any payments. Discuss your plans for meeting your payment schedule and explore mutually acceptable ways to solve your temporary setback.

6. *Verify your credit upgrade.* Once you fulfill your side of the bargain, your credit should be in good shape. Order

an updated copy of your credit file to verify that the creditor has honored his agreement to make the promised changes. Allow for a reasonable time before you request your update. If the changes have not been made, immediately remind the creditor of his agreement. If the creditor still refuses to make the agreed changes, you can then dispute the information on your credit report using the creditor's agreement to support the change.

Put your bad credit in a good light

Despite your best efforts, you can't always erase negative credit information from your credit report. But you can always file a statement to explain the circumstances that led to your bad credit. You accomplish this by sending the credit bureau a consumer statement of 100 words or less which is then incorporated into your credit report and sent together with your credit report to any prospective creditor.

A statement in your credit report gives other creditors your side of the story and you can greatly mitigate the damage from negative credit information.

Your consumer statement should give the situation that led to the negative mark the most favorable light possible. For example, an entry that you filed Chapter 13 bankruptcy becomes considerably softened by a consumer statement that you eventually paid your creditors 100 percent of what you owed. Or a rash of late-pay entries may be satisfactorily explained by documenting an illness that prevented you from working. This becomes even less a credit problem if your consumer statement further points out that you have punctually paid before and after the sickness.

Make certain the credit bureau publishes the entire statement. Some credit bureaus shorten statements that are less than 100 words. This is illegal. You can submit a longer consumer statement, but the credit bureau can then reduce the statement to 100 words. However, it must then help you summarize the statement within the 100-word limit. If the credit bureau tells you that it will put a copy of your consumer statement in your file, demand that it be incorporated as part of your credit report, and literally become attached to it. No one will journey to the bureau to look up your statement. They will only consider it if it is on the report they read. The credit bureau also may ask you to select a "prewritten" statement. Refuse! Insist upon drafting your own statement. Remember, you have a legal right to draft your own personal consumer statement and have it become part of your credit report.

Do not understate the power of the consumer statement. It has one purpose—to convince prospective creditors that the problems of the past won't be repeated in the future. This is the essence of credit repair.

Here are some examples of good consumer statements.

1) Upon moving to Florida from Ohio, I notified XYZ department store to send my statements to my new address. I notified XYZ four times that I was not receiving my statements. It took six months for me to get my statements from XYZ and this is why I did not pay them.

    Dated_____

    Signed_____

2) It did not occur to me that XYZ was reporting my account as a charge off to the credit bureau. I have offered repeatedly to pay the bill in full if XYZ will agree to remove the false and misleading information from my report. I continue to be punished because of their incompetence.

    Dated_____

    Signed_____

3) I purchased faulty merchandise from XYZ department store just before that branch closed down. My letters to the company were never answered. When I finally reached a supervisor on the phone, he said too much time had elapsed and nothing could be done. I refused to continue paying on the account until a settlement was made. The company ignored my request and reported my account as a charge off. Even though I paid off the balance, they refuse to remove the charge off.

Dated_____

Signed_____

4) My business had maintained a banking relationship for 12 years with XYZ bank. I trusted every manager to understand the nature of the local economy which had good times and bad times. The current manager has refused to acknowledge the current downswing in the local economy, my divorce and recent serious illness. He has charged off my loan of $7,500 and will not even discuss this with me. Having ruined credit, my business has failed but my creditors have succeeded.

Dated_____

Signed_____

5) Three years ago I bought a used car from XYZ motor corporation and faithfully made every monthly payment. Unfortunately, I became seriously ill, was hospitalized for three weeks, and was then confined to bed for four weeks before I could resume my job. XYZ repossessed my car after I informed them that I would have to miss a second payment. I offered to make extra payments as soon as I returned to work. They refused to listen. I have a good job and another car but my credit is ruined.

Dated_____

Signed_____

6) Your Address

Date

Credit Bureau Name

Credit Bureau Address

To whom it may concern:

On June 8, 1994 I sent you a letter disputing information in my credit report regarding XYZ department store. On July 9, 1994 I received notice from you that you would not remove the disputed information because XYZ verified the accuracy of the information. I now demand that you include the following consumer statement in my credit report because the information you supposedly verified remains incorrect.

On December 3,1993, I purchased a computer form XYZ department store. The salesman said that if I opened a charge account with the store, I would receive a 10 percent discount on that purchase. I did this. The computer never worked properly and the store refused to exchange it or refund my money. The next day I left the computer with the department manager and never made any payments. XYZ reported my account as a charge off.

Under 15 U.S.C. ß1681i(b), you must include this statement in any consumer report that contains this disputed information. In addition, because this statement contains less than 100 words, I demand that the full text of this statement be included without alteration.

Thank you for your attention to this matter.

Sincerely,

_____

Key points to remember:

- Many banks use a point scoring system to grant or deny credit. The higher your score, the better your chances for obtaining credit

- Know your five legal rights under the Fair Credit Reporting Act.

- When you receive your report examine it very carefully.

- Remove the "credit killers" from your report by following the seven basic steps to credit repair. You may repeat the process as often as three times before moving on to advanced techniques.

- Try contacting and negotiating directly with the creditor when your creditor stands behind his credit entry.

- Use the 100-word consumer statement. Never underestimate its power.

- Do not contact the credit bureau by telephone. That's a wasted effort. Put it in writing and keep copies of all written communication with the credit bureaus.

- Do not become impatient. Do not give up. Persevere!

More Surefire Credit Repair Strategies

4

More Surefire Credit Repair Strategies

Despite your best efforts to clear your credit, some bad marks may remain. In this chapter you will learn the advanced strategies and techniques for removing those stubborn, unyielding negatives on your credit report—tax liens, foreclosures and repossessions, bankruptcy, and judgments. Because these credit killers reflect legal actions undertaken either by yourself or your creditors, they are public record and are then considerably more difficult to delete from your credit report than are late payments or unpaid bills. But these nasty credit killers can be removed from your credit report if you understand the law of obsolescence and the principle of verification—and how to apply each.

So where do you start? Again put your credit record through the credit repair process before you proceed to these advanced strategies.

Removing obsolete information from your credit report

Negative information on your credit report may be obsolete or on your credit report for longer than allowed under the Fair Credit Reporting Act.

The law sets a statutory time period, or number of years, a credit bureau can report bad credit information. Without this time limitation a credit bureau could keep negative information on your record forever.

A credit bureau *must* delete obsolete information from your credit report. However, you cannot always rely on a credit bureau to delete obsolete information on its own. So, you must carefully review your credit report to determine which negative marks are obsolete and removable. You must then notify the credit bureau to remove them.

What are the statutory time limits for reporting negative credit information?

1) ***Poor payment history.*** Credit bureaus can generally report credit delinquencies for seven years. This includes reports of late or non-payment as well as collection or charge-off reports. Most negative marks are subject to the seven-year rule.

Unfortunately, it is not always easy to determine when the seven years begins, and hence, become obsolete. The Federal Trade Commission says the time period runs from the date of the last activity on your account. But this could be when you made your last payment, or it may be later, such as when the creditor made his last collection effort. Once your creditor charged-off your account, you do not restart or extend the statute of limitations by making a later payment.

As a basic rule, all negative credit information against you, except for the items below, are subject to the seven-year reporting rule.

2) ***Credit transaction involving more than $50,000 in principal.*** While a credit bureau must generally delete adverse credit information that is over seven years old, the credit bureau can forever disclose any adverse credit information on a credit transaction involving more than $50,000 in principal. For instance, you apply for a $100,000 mortgage, a prospective creditor can see your entire credit file from the beginning of time. Obviously, stale credit information should not adversely influence a new creditor if your current credit is good.

3) *Life insurance over $50,000.* As with credit over $50,000, a credit bureau can report adverse credit information of any age to an insurance company checking your credit for life insurance with a face value of $50,000 or more.

4) *Employment with an annual salary over $20,000.* A credit bureau also can report bad credit information that is obsolete to a prospective employer who may offer you a job that pays $20,000 a year or more. Because most salaries exceed this amount, many Americans face disclosure of their early credit history.

Although these are three situations where a credit bureau can report obsolete credit information, credit bureaus normally do not keep obsolete credit information in their files.

5) *Lawsuits and judgments.* Credit bureaus can report lawsuits or judgments against you for seven years from date of entry. However, this can be extended to the length of time a judgment remains in force under state law. In many states this is 20 years, so the judgment may remain on your credit record for that time.

6) *Bankruptcy.* Bankruptcy can stay on your credit record for 10 years from the date of filing (not the date of discharge). In practice, credit bureaus usually report Chapter 13 wage-earner plans for seven years, and only Chapter 7 bankruptcies for ten years.

7) *Tax liens.* An unpaid IRS tax lien also can be reported for 10 years from the date of filing. A paid tax lien can stay on your record for seven years from the date of final payment.

8) *Arrest, indictment, or conviction.* Credit bureaus can report arrests, indictments or conviction of a crime for seven years from the date of disposition, release or parole, whichever occurs last.

How do you delete obsolete information from your credit report?

Once you identify obsolete items on your credit report, you must write the credit bureaus to delete them. Sample letters are contained in this book.

Enforce your rights! If an entry is obsolete (beyond the time limit within which the information can legally be on your credit report), then the credit bureau *must* delete it from your record.

Document your case so the credit bureau sees that the information is obsolete. Document when the statute of limitations began so the credit bureau can readily determine the information is obsolete and therefore require deletion from your credit report.

The credit bureau should acknowledge that it is deleting the obsolete information within 30 days. Request your updated report to make certain it is deleted.

What if the credit bureau refuses to delete obsolete information? Threaten the bureau with a legal suit for damages and a complaint to the Federal Trade Commission. You should always be prepared to follow through.

If the credit bureau does not reply within 30 days of your written protest, you can then additionally demand deletion due to a late or tardy reply.

How to erase the credit killers from your credit file

Late-pay or no-pay entries on your credit report can seriously hurt your credit. But four credit killers can destroy your chances for any significant credit. These credit killers are:

- Tax liens
- Foreclosures and repossessions
- Bankruptcy
- Judgments

And if these credit killers on your credit report are current and accurate, how then can you possibly remove them from your current report?

The technique is to once again exploit the fact that a credit bureau must verify all disputed entries within 30 days, or alternatively delete the negative entry on your credit report.

This is how credit repair companies effectively repair their clients' credit. When they find a bankruptcy, tax lien, foreclosure or judgment on the credit report, they simply protest the entry. They rely on the probability that the credit bureau cannot verify the information within 30 days, and is then forced to delete the information from the credit report. The success odds increase considerably if the credit bureau receives protests on a number of entries. So your protest does not appear frivolous, dispute only one item in each letter. However, you can send any number of separate letters at approximately the same time.

Why may this work? Consider what happens in practice.

- **Tax liens.** Assume you deny owing the IRS and therefore dispute a tax lien. The credit bureau must notify the IRS for verification. But it's useful to know that after about two years your tax records are held in the federal archives, so the chances of the IRS verifying your tax liability within the required 30 days is quite small. The tax lien must then be deleted.

- **Foreclosure or repossession.** Consider the many ways you can dispute a foreclosure or repossession. Perhaps you were only a guarantor on the loan. Or maybe you only voluntarily surrendered the collateral to the lender. Or you may have fully paid the loan balance so the lender suffered no loss. The mere entry of a foreclosure against you would then be misleading and disputable. The odds are again good that the lender, if challenged, will not verify the foreclosure entry.

- **Bankruptcy.** It is more difficult, but still possible, to dispute a bankruptcy. For example, you may have filed a Chapter 13 wage-earner plan or a Chapter 11 reorganization, which is different than a Chapter 7 bankruptcy. You see the point. Take advantage of whatever technicalities you can. Like the IRS, bankruptcy courts dead store their files after a year or two, and, as with any bureaucracy, cannot easily verify the information in a short 30 days. And since your original creditors won't get any money out of you, they probably won't search their dead files to establish the bankruptcy filing.

Creditors also may have trouble verifying the debt because the judgement amount and the amount of the original debt won't match. The final judgment probably includes attorney's fees, interest and other collection fees. The burden of proof truly becomes burdensome when the creditor must verify the amount of the judgment.

It is important to get the negative account entries removed *before* you try to remove the bankruptcy itself. If you can remove the individual accounts that led to the bankruptcy, the bankruptcy would then be unverifiable, and must be removed. Once an account is deleted, it is deleted forever from the bureau's files. The bureau would have no record of the creditor's action and cannot then contact that creditor to legally verify the debt. It is as though the creditor and the debt never existed. In the process, you have effectively removed the legal underpinnings of the bankruptcy. Since it would be prohibitively expensive and involve many attorney hours for the bureau to verify the bankruptcy under these conditions, the bankruptcy also must be removed from your credit report.

Another effective strategy: Turn your bankruptcy file into a "missing file" which works well if your bankruptcy is at least two years old. It's not difficult. First dispute your bankruptcy with the credit bureau. Then wait one week after mailing the dispute letter and go to the court where your bankruptcy was filed to review your file. It will, of course, take a couple of weeks to retrieve the records from the federal archives. You will be notified by the clerk of the court that your records have arrived.

Do nothing until the clerk of the court threatens to send your records back to the federal archives, then request an extension. Your bankruptcy records will be placed in a special area where they will continue to remain out of circulation. Finally, you will now have tied up your bankruptcy files and taken them out of circulation for several weeks and this may prevent the credit bureau from meeting the 30 day deadline.

- **Judgments.** There are a number of ways to contest a judgment. Was it paid or discharged in bankruptcy? Did the creditor release you from the debt? Is the amount incorrect?

One perfectly legal and effective strategy you can use to remove any judgement from your credit report is to get the court to vacate or void the judgment. There are three situations when a court will vacate a judgement:

1) Excusable neglect
2) Mistake
3) Newly discovered material evidence

To begin the process, file a "motion to vacate" with the court. This is not complex. You simply fill out a form. To have the motion granted, you must prove that the judgement was based upon excusable neglect, mistake, or new evidence has been discovered which should reverse the entry of a judgment against you.

1) **Excusable neglect.** This is the most common reason a judgment is vacated. Excusable neglect occurs when procedural circumstances clearly beyond your control result in a default judgment against you. What circumstances provide excusable neglect? Perhaps your failure to act was due to a clerical or secretarial error which prevented a timely defense. A serious delay in the mail may have prevented you from replying to a matter on time. Did your spouse fail to inform you, as a co-defendant, about the complaint? Sometimes excusable neglect results from a misunderstanding. You may have believed an earlier but related case you were involved in protected your rights. Did you fail to appear in court

because of a physical or mental illness? Again, excusable neglect. If you hired an attorney and reasonably relied on his representing you in court but found instead that he was called away to attend an emergency or that his secretary erred in the court date, you have excusable neglect. Did you live in another state and were not given enough time to hire an out-of-state attorney? Often, excusable neglect results from confusion or misunderstanding. Perhaps you failed to inquire as to whether your insurance company was, in fact, responsible for paying the claim.

You get the idea. Excusable neglect results from your good intentions gone astray. They have been sabotaged by circumstances beyond your control—misplaced trust, miscommunication, unavoidable delays, injuries, sickness or misunderstandings. Any one of these may have resulted in the default judgement against you. These are persuasive arguments to have the judgment vacated.

2) **Mistake.** Go back and carefully read each document you received from the court when the judgment was entered against you. Did the clerk of the court make a mistake with the paperwork? Was the amount wrong? Were the names of the parties reversed? Was the case dismissed prior to judgment? Did the party suing you actually drop or withdraw the suit prior to judgment? You get the idea. See if you can find an error in how the judgment was recorded, entered, or filed with the court. If you can find cause, then you can file a "motion to vacate" based on mistake.

3) **Newly discovered evidence.** This evidence can be anything that would prove to the court that you did not owe the debt in the first place. Some affirmative defenses that you might discover are that the plaintiff was not legally entitled to do business in your state because it had not registered to do so, or was not legally entitled or licensed to sell the product or perform the service. Possibly the contract was illegal, that you were under age at the time, or the contract was usurious.

A final method of getting the judgment vacated is to strike a deal with the creditor. Offer to pay the judgment in exchange for the creditor's willingness to vacate it.

If you do succeed in vacating the judgment, send a copy of the court order to the credit bureau and request that the bureau delete it from your credit report. The credit bureau must comply.

Bankruptcies, liens, foreclosures and judgments are public records. Public records usually list you by name and social security number. If the social security number on your credit report fails to match the public records, the debt cannot be identified. A simple error of even one digit of your social security number by a recording secretary will prevent your bankruptcy from being identified. This is why liens and judgments, for example, occasionally fail to turn up on credit reports. They do not match.

The key to success in each of these instances is to hold the credit bureau to the 30-day deadline. Unless it can verify the information within 30 days, you must insist that the unverified information be deleted. You will find effective letters to help you at the end of this book.

Erasing bad credit marks by taking advantage of the 30-day verification provision has its limitations.

First, government agencies—such as the IRS and bankruptcy courts—are beginning to recognize their vulnerability as bureaucracies with neither the ability nor incentive to swiftly reply. This is changing. Computerized records now make it much easier for these agencies to retrieve records and reply rapidly to any challenges.

Second, the credit bureau may simply modify the credit information according to your protest, rather than completely delete it. For example, if you claim to have paid a judgment, the credit report may simply note the judgment was paid. While this is preferable to an unpaid judgment, it does not accomplish your objective of completely erasing reference to the judgment. To achieve that, you must use a vague protest which only disputes the entry.

Third, the credit bureau may consider your protest frivolous. If the credit bureau has reason to believe your protest is frivolous or made in bad faith, it can disregard the 30-day rule. This is the credit bureau's loophole when it has good cause to believe you are abusing the system. How do you avoid this? Don't challenge too many negatives at one time. Attack them singly. Also be vague to the point the credit bureau cannot modify your entry. Finally, do not use form letters or boiler plate correspondence which gives your letters an assembly line appearance.

Key points to remember

- Repeat the basic credit repair process at least twice before you move on to more advanced credit repair techniques.

- A credit bureau must, by law, delete obsolete information from your report. But never rely on the bureau to do so on its own.

- Learn when information becomes obsolete so that you may effectively protest those items.

- Always document your case.

- "Credit Killers" such as tax liens, foreclosures, repossessions, bankruptcies, and judgments can be removed from your credit file.

- The credit bureau must verify a disputed entry within 30 days or remove it from your report.

- Be careful not to use form letters when you correspond with the credit bureau.

- Do not flood the credit bureau with disputes. They may then consider it "frivolous and irrelevant."

- Your credit cannot be quickly rebuilt. Be patient. Never allow yourself to become discouraged.

How To Build Triple-A Credit

5

How To Build
Triple-A Credit

Just as it is possible to turn poor credit into good credit, if you now have fair credit you can as easily enjoy great credit! Yes, triple A credit can be yours—within 90 days—if you know the secrets.

Previous chapters showed you how to repair your credit. That is the all-important first step to triple-A credit because it eliminates those negative comments that shout that you are a poor credit risk. But even when this is accomplished, you, at best, get only neutral credit. Nothing in your credit report convinces a prospective lender that you are that good credit risk that deserves credit. If your credit report justifies some credit, why not build your credit-power so you get *all* of the credit you need?

That's what triple-A credit is all about. Triple-A credit gets you credit 100 percent of the time, for any purpose, and for the maximum amount you can safely repay.

How creditors measure your credit power

How do prospective creditors measure your credit power? Credit managers, whether in department stores or banks, chiefly rely on three indicators to determine your credit power:

1) Capacity
2) Collateral

3) Character

These "three c's of credit" show prospective creditors your:

- "Capacity" or income to pay the debt
- "Collateral" or assets to secure the obligation
- "Character" or willingness to promptly repay the debt

Capacity

The first question is whether you have sufficient income to repay the debt. Creditors will check to see if your income exceeds your expenses so that you can comfortably pay the debt. A creditor will then want to know:

1) Your income—from all sources
2) Your fixed expenses
3) Your other debts

The amount remaining from your total net income, after deducting your fixed monthly expenses and other debts, is your capacity. If your net income (after taxes) is $2,000 a month and your total living expenses (rent, food, clothing, medical, etc.) is $1,500, then your credit capacity is an amount that requires no more than $500 in monthly payments. If you now pay $400 a month for other credit obligations, then your remaining capacity is $100 a month, and a creditor should extend you that amount of credit.

You can then easily maximize your credit power in three ways:

- Increase your income
- Decrease your expenses
- Reduce your other debts

Increase your income

Creditors prefer to see a high income because this gives you more disposable income—or capacity—to pay your debts. You also appear more stable or responsible than a low-income earner. While this is not always true, high income does nevertheless imply creditworthiness.

Perhaps you cannot get a higher paying job, but you may boost your income by reporting your overtime pay, bonuses, and anticipated raises in the year ahead.

Your salary may only be a part of your income. Don't forget to tell a creditor about your:

- Commissions
- Interest
- Dividends
- Rents
- Royalties
- Alimony and support
- Governmental subsidies
- Social Security

Do you have other sources of income? Are you expecting repayment of a debt, an inheritance or settlement on a legal case? A creditor will less willingly extend credit against this type of income because it represents uncertain or contingent income. However, the expectation of income from these sources may easily tip the credit decision in your favor.

Are you planning to sell a major asset—such as a house, car or boat—to help purchase something you want to finance? Let the creditor know the loan will be repaid from these proceeds rather than from your income. Be prepared to show the creditor that you can sell the item quickly enough to repay the loan. This is particularly important if you cannot comfortably repay the loan from your income.

Your earnings are only one factor. Creditors also consider the stability of your income. Your occupation is an important factor when obtaining credit because it directly influences your stability. Certain occupations are less stable than others. A tenured school teacher certainly has more secure employment than does a construction worker or commissioned salesperson. When you fill out a credit application you should creatively camouflage your job title or description if you fall into any of the following occupations:

- Actor
- Amusement park employee
- Bartender
- Beautician
- Cook
- Flea market vendor
- Gas station attendant
- Hospital orderly
- Hotel employee
- House painter
- Laborer
- Musician
- Nurse's assistant
- Porter
- Practical nurse
- Retiree
- Self employed
- Taxi driver
- Unskilled factory worker
- Waiter/waitress
- Any occupation with the word "freelance" or "student"

These are not considered negative occupations "creditwise," if you list them as part-time sources of extra income.

From a stability point of view your application also may automatically trigger suspicions if:

- Your business and residence addresses are the same
- You live in a residence hotel
- You use a mail drop
- You are employed by a new business
- You have a recent drug conviction
- You are a non-citizen

- You have many recent address changes
- You have too many credit cards for your income

Length of time on the job evidences both job stability and personal stability. Most lenders want a credit applicant employed in the same job for at least one year, and with reasonably steady employment for the prior five years.

Be prepared to explain frequent job interruptions. Did you voluntarily leave your employment? Were you self-employed during these intervals, perhaps as a consultant? Were you unemployed due to a business closing?

Creditors want assurances that your income will continue so you can pay your obligations. Paint that picture. For long term loans, you must convince the creditor that your job has long-term stability. If your employer is a small business, the creditor may check its financial stability. If you are self-employed, the lender may want financial statements on your business.

Do you plan on changing jobs? Then apply for credit before you change jobs. That's when you will have the benefit of job stability.

Credit applications do not always give you sufficient space to explain your job history. Attach a brief explanation, for instance, that you changed jobs frequently to consistently advance, or that your position was terminated due to a plant shutdown, or you returned to school, or had a stint in the military, or had medical problems. Creditors understand. Think like a creditor!

Decrease your expenses

Credit applications generally have you list your major expenses. If your expenses are too high compared to your income, you may not have enough money each month to repay your loan. In other words, you have no credit capacity.

Reconstruct your monthly budget. How much money remains after you pay your usual living expenses? You may not be able to significantly increase your income but you probably can tighten your belt and reduce your expenses to increase your credit capacity.

- Where can you economize and lower your expenses?
- Do you have expenses others can share?
- Do you have expenses that will soon end (college tuition, etc.)?

Here are some expense-reduction strategies:

1) **Alternative living arrangements.** If you can share a house or an apartment you will save rent and also share utilities and lower your monthly housing expenditures.

2) **Food.** Bring your own lunch to work. Eat out less often and share food expenses by eating more meals with family and friends. Become a smart food shopper and use coupons to save money.

3) **Clothing.** Clothing expenses can be reduced by designing a multi-purpose wardrobe, watching for sales, and buying "quality."

4) **Telephone.** Its costs can be dramatically reduced by buying your phone instead of leasing it, reducing the number of phones, using a cheaper long distance carrier, and by carefully examining your phone bills for improper charges. Do not pay for optional services that aren't absolutely necessary, or make unnecessary long-distance phone calls.

Reduce your other debts

Creditors do not always share the same yardstick when determining whether you have too much debt. But most creditors do not want your monthly debt payments (exclusive of your mortgage payment) to exceed 20 percent of your gross or pre-tax income. For example, if your gross income is $5,000 a month, a lender will not want your other debts payments to exceed $1,000. But that is only a rough rule-of-thumb. Creditors will also consider many other factors:

- Your monthly expenses
- Whether your income is likely to increase
- Whether other debts will soon be paid

- Whether you historically had that debt level and still paid your obligations promptly

Apply for new credit after you paid an existing obligation. A new lender will be more hesitant to lend if you are already heavily indebted.

Do not be tempted into omitting certain debts from your credit application. Expect your creditor to check your credit report. If your "deleted" credit accounts then appear on your report it will only throw your honesty and integrity into question and this will certainly hurt your chances for credit. If, for any reason, you plan to delete an account from your credit application, then do review your credit reports beforehand to make certain the "deleted account" does not appear. Always list accounts that do appear.

It is important to know three additional rules banks and mortgage lenders use when measuring the reasonableness of your credit request.

1) **The 10 percent rule.** This rule, used by lenders to determine what you can safely handle in monthly payments, especially applies to first time applicants. The rule simply states that your monthly payments should not exceed 10 percent of your monthly net income. If your monthly net income is $1,500, your monthly loan payments should be $150, or less. If your outstanding loans exceed 10 percent, you have far less chance of having another loan approved.

2) **The 28 percent rule.** This rule, usually applied to home mortgage applications, states that your monthly mortgage payments should not exceed 28 percent of your gross income. This rule is chiefly used when you have no other debts, such as credit card debts or automobile loans.

3) **The 36 percent rule.** This rule states that the mortgage, combined with all other debt, must not exceed 36 percent of your annual gross income. This is not monthly payments but total debt.

Collateral

A lender can be secured or unsecured. Secured creditors hold a lien against specific assets, such as real estate, a car, or boat. If you fail to pay, the secured lender can sell the pledged asset to recover payment. This, of course, is a safe loan for a lender— provided the pledged asset can be sold by the lender for an amount that will cover the loan balance. Secured lenders seldom loan more than the auction value of the collateral.

Secured credit, is an almost guaranteed way to rebuild your credit. Even with poor credit, a lender may advance you credit if you can secure the credit with a lien against some valuable asset. Many lenders extend credit entirely on the strength of the pledged assets. Other credit considerations are either ignored or carry comparatively little weight in the credit decision.

When you have bad credit you may have to rebuild your credit through a series of secured loans. Prove your creditworthiness with secured obligations and you can apply for an unsecured loan.

Unsecured creditors, of course, do not enjoy the same strong position as a secured creditor. An unsecured lender cannot simply seize an asset if you don't pay, but must first sue on his claim and win a judgment. Only then can the lender seize your assets.

However, if you have no assets, or if they are already pledged to another lender, then the unsecured lender has no effective recourse, notwithstanding his judgment.

Still unsecured creditors do consider the value of your assets. Unsecured creditors see significant assets as a sign of financial stability. And when the assets significantly exceed the borrower's liabilities, the lender seeks excess assets to satisfy a judgment.

Securing your debt by pledging assets almost always get you credit faster and easier than unsecured borrowing. You will also get more credit.

What can you use as collateral to secure your debts and rebuild your credit? You may be appreciably wealthier than you think. Add the value of your various assets (property that you own) and subtract any existing mortgages or liens against those assets. The difference is your equity or net worth in the asset. This is what you have available to secure a loan.

Don't overlook any asset:

- Home
- Investment real estate
- Stocks, bonds, mutual funds
- Automobile
- Boats, planes, recreational vehicles
- Notes and mortgages due you
- Art, jewelry, antiques
- Pensions, IRAs and Keoghs
- Royalty income
- Income from trusts

You may have other assets to pledge. The point is that collateral gives you a borrowing power approximately equal to your equity in your assets. Regardless of your credit history, if you have collateral worth a solid $100,000, you should be able to borrow close to that amount. And when listing an asset, do list its current value, not what you originally paid for it. Creditors prefer liquid assets, such as a pledged bankbook or securities, because these assets are easily liquidated. Creditors also are interested in high-value, tangible assets such as a home or automobiles.

Many credit applications ask about your bank accounts, but rarely does a bank ask how much you have in other bank accounts. The only information a bank can get from another bank is account verification. Banks cannot disclose how much money is in your account. So it is a smart idea to open several small bank accounts in banks other than the bank you target for a loan. Multiple bank accounts in multiple banks maximizes your perceived wealth.

Character

Creditors next consider your character. How important this is depends upon the type credit, and who your creditors are. Asset-based lenders rely chiefly on collateral, and they are less concerned with your character than are unsecured creditors who can only rely on your prior reliability for honoring your obligations.

In the credit world "character" means the probability you will honor your future obligations, which is based on how you have honored past obligations. But creditors do look beyond past credit problems. They also want to know:

1) How many credit defaults have you had? What was the reason for the defaults? How recent are they?

2) Do you own your own home?

3) If you rent, for how long have you rented the same apartment or house?

4) Do you have a checking account?

5) Do you have a savings account with regular deposits?

6) Do you have a payroll savings plan at work?

7) Do you have a telephone in your own name?

8) Do you have a criminal record?

9) Have you filed bankruptcy?

Creditors look for patterns. It is less likely that a creditor will find a negative pattern if you have few recent credit defaults. It is an extremely positive sign if you continued to own your own home despite financial difficulties, or you recently purchased a home and promptly made all the mortgage payments. Renting at the same location for a number of years also demonstrates stability. Other creditors consider financial stability a checking and savings account fed with regular deposits. Of course, as a responsible applicant, you should also have a telephone in your own name to further evidence your financial stability.

Positive answers to these nine questions will often offset an otherwise negative credit report. Obviously, it shall also depend a great deal on how poor your credit now is. Essentially, the lender must believe that you will remain in town to repay your loan, that you practice sound credit management, and that you are now stable, responsible, and productive.

When you are denied credit

If your credit application has been denied, the Equal Credit Opportunity Act entitles you to know why. If the creditor doesn't supply you with the reason, ask for it. The Federal Reserve Board lists these 20-most-common-reasons for credit rejection:

1) Your credit application was incomplete.

2) You had too few credit references.

3) Your credit references could not be verified.

4) You had no credit file.

5) Your credit file had insufficient information.

6) You have delinquent credit obligations.

7) You have not been employed for an adequate time.

8) Your employment has been irregular.

9) Your employment cannot be verified.

10) You have insufficient income.

11) Your income cannot be verified.

12) You have too many debts.

13) You have insufficient collateral.

14) You have lived too briefly at your present address.

15) Your current residence is temporary.

16) Your current residence cannot be verified.

17) Your wages are currently garnished or attached.

18) You have a foreclosure, bankruptcy, or repossession on your recent record.

19) You are engaged in a lawsuit.

20) The creditor does not grant credit to any applicant on the terms requested, or offer the type loan you requested. (Before you deal with any prospective

creditor, make sure that the creditor offers the type credit you want. If you want an unsecured loan, why waste time with a lender that does not make this type of loan?)

This list highlights the many possible obstacles to credit. If you foresee one or more of these problems, then attach a note of explanation to your application. Anticipating problems is one important weapon. An explanation before you are rejected may effectively diffuse the problem. Consider these points when you talk to your creditor. Never ignore them! Your creditor won't.

You can always appeal once you know why your credit was rejected. Discuss the problems with the creditor. The creditor should willingly tell you what you must to do to qualify for credit. Always approach your creditor in a friendly, candid and courteous manner. Don't be antagonistic. Remember, the creditor must sense that you feel creditworthy and can repay the debt. Be both persistent and concerned about why your application was not approved. Find out what actions you can take and what other information you could furnish for your application to be approved. Then re-submit a revised application.

Flexing your credit-power

An important first step in building credit is to open a checking account and a savings account at a local bank or credit union. Pick a bank that reports credit transactions to the credit bureaus.

The second step? Open utility accounts in your name. Gas, electric, and telephone bills paid monthly and reported to the credit bureaus will quickly energize your credit.

The third step is to actually obtain credit. Use your savings account as collateral. You may borrow dollar for dollar with a passbook loan. This type loan works well with as little as $500. Once you secure a loan with a passbook, you cannot touch the funds until you have fully repaid the loan. So make sure you can do without these funds for at least 30 days.

A bank secured with your passbook has no risk in lending you money, so any bank should be willing. It is extremely important that the bank or credit union reports consumer loans to the credit bureau. If your bank does not, select another bank. The purpose of these credit building exercises is to pepper good reports on your credit report.

Once you do borrow money, repay the entire loan amount in 25 days. Because you have fully repaid the loan before it was due, the bank or credit union will send a positive entry to your credit bureau Continue to deposit regularly to your savings account to build your balance and qualify for even larger loans. Establish a wider field of credit. Include several banks or credit unions for maximum effect.

How to parlay $1000 into a millionaire's credit

You don't have to be a millionaire to enjoy truly powerful credit. You can build powerful credit with as little as $1000. Here's how. With the $1,000 in your account, ask the loan officer for a twelve-month $1000 passbook loan. Although you can achieve this with less money, $1,000 is the loan category where you earn a high rating from the credit bureau. Explain to your lenders that the higher interest on your outstanding debts justifies borrowing to pay these debts. Under these circumstances most banks will not run a credit check before giving you the loan.

With your additional loan, open a savings account at another bank with the $1,000 loan received from the first bank. Then request that they give you a $1,000 12-month loan, but do not mention the loan received from the first bank. Wait a week or two and repeat the process at a third bank: Deposit the $1,000 you received from the second bank into a savings account, and later get still another $1,000 12-month secured loan.

Next, at one of the three banks, open a checking account with the $1,000 you received from the third bank. You now have $1,000 in a checking account and three outstanding 12-month loans at three different banks—for a total of $3,000. Deduct your original $1,000 and you need only repay $2,000 plus interest. But make certain that no loan carries a prepayment penalty.

Finally, about one week later start to pre-pay your three loans. You will then have an advance payment record with three banks and will have established powerful credit for your credit report. Merchant and entertainment credit cards and even unsecured bankcards will soon be yours for the asking!

This proven strategy can help you establish limited credit in a relatively short time using few lending institutions. You still have over $3,000 in debt to repay in 12 months. But if you can handle this, you will find this is a fast and practical technique to rebuild stronger credit.

Great credit in only 30 days

Here's another credit-building technique that was originally developed for undercover FBI agents who needed to quickly establish a positive credit history. The method originally involved banks where you previously established credit. But you need not be an FBI agent. Today it is used by those with no credit, or poor credit but who have friends or relatives with excellent credit. Here's how it works:

Have a trusted friend or relative with good credit and a bankcard request that their bank issue a second card in your name. This second card issued to you will have a different account number with the original signer of the account the guarantor. The credit bureau will then report the entire history of the original card's credit transactions on your report. The credit history will include the date the account was opened and the entire payment record. However, it will not say your credit report is based on a secondary card and your credit report will remain completely independent with excellent credit.

If you must complete a credit application for the secondary card, then have the cardholder complete it under the co-applicant category.

It is smart to use secured credit cards and co-signers to help you establish credit. Borrow and repay quickly and you win the credit you need for larger and larger loans. But you must use lenders that report to credit bureaus, because this is the only way these positive credit entries land on your credit report. Never miss a payment, and never default on a loan or you will have destroyed everything you have worked so hard to achieve.

Three dishonest credit practices to avoid

Other tactics can help you build credit, but may be illegal. Although commonly used, you must never use them fraudulently. Beware these schemes. They can only get you into trouble:

1) *Computer generated secondary credit report.* The nature of data entry and retrieval allows computers to search your file by code or file numbers. Computers do not search word by word for your file. Rather than search first for your last name, first name, middle initial, current street, town, state, or social security number, codes are instead assigned to the searches. The first two initials or numbers of the target entry usually are sufficient to retrieve your file. These letters and numbers, strung together, produce the code.

These codes not only pull up your file but also other files that closely match the code. For example, if your name is John Smith and your address is 6259 Beaverbrook Road, Lashdale, New Mexico 63207 and your social security number is 023 45 6789, your code might look something like this: JOSM62BERDLANM63023. But if the computer cannot find a close enough match because too few digits match, it will not pull alternate files and make substitutions. The computer will simply state that there is no record of that person. If the computer was instructed to find JOSM6BERDLANM0? It would come up empty. However, at that point the request will generate a new file. The new file would be JOSM6BERDLANM0, and as a new file would have no credit history.

Such reports are frequently generated accidentally. Now what if you cannot remember your exact social security number and you accidentally omit a number, or perhaps omit a number from your zip code? You may have started a secondary file.

You can change the order and number of digits by creating new addresses, using friend's addresses, or by using mail drops. The links that most influence the computer's search, however, are name, social security number, address and zip code.

The applicant must keep an exact record of these changes when requesting the credit report from the credit bureau. The applicant might give his correct name, but with the new address as the current address and a still different address as the prior address.

If the result is a "no report available," then you have confirmed the creation of a secondary file and you can start a new credit history.

To avoid dealing directly with the credit bureau, one can use credit applications to do the work. Applying for merchant credit cards, or more easily-obtained credit cards until you receive a "no record" response, also confirms there is a secondary file. The secondary file becomes your primary file for credit reporting purposes and the old file will eventually be eliminated through disuse.

2) *Skin shedding.* This simply involves creating an entirely new identity. Two systems are commonly used to achieve new identities. The first changes the social security numbers. For instance, find the name of a child with a similar birthday as yours, someone who perhaps died 10-20 years earlier. Obtain that child's social security number and you have a new identity.

Here's what you must first know about social security numbers:

- No social security numbers have been issued with consecutive zeros.
- Beginning numbers 700-728 are reserved for railroad employees.
- The first three digits identify geographical areas:

001-003	New Hampshire	501-502	N. Dakota
004-007	Maine	503-504	S. Dakota
008-009	Vermont	505-508	Nebraska
010-034	Massachusetts	509-515	Kansas
035-039	Rhode Island	516-517	Montana
040-049	Connecticut	518-519	Idaho
050-134	New York	520	Wyoming
135-158	New Jersey	521-524	Colorado
159-211	Pennsylvania	525	New Mexico
212-220	Maryland	526-527	Arizona
221-222	Delaware	528-529	Utah
223-231	Virginia	530	Nevada
232-236	W. Virginia	531-539	Washington
	N. Carolina	540-544	Oregon
237-246	N Carolina	545-573	California
247-251	S. Carolina	574	Alaska
252-260	Georgia	575-576	Hawaii
261-267	Florida	577-579	D.C.
268-302	Ohio	580	Virgin Islands
303-317	Indiana	580-584	Puerto Rico
318-361	Illinois	585	New Mexico
387-399	Wisconsin	586	Guam
400-407	Kentucky		Am. Samoa
408-415	Tennessee		Philippines
416-424	Alabama	587-588	Mississippi
425-428	Mississippi	589-595	Florida
429-432	Arkansas	596-599	Puerto Rico
433-439	Louisiana	600-601	Arizona
440-448	Oklahoma	602-626	California
449-467	Texas	627-645	Texas
468-477	Minnesota	646-647	Utah
478-485	Iowa	648-649	New Mexico
486-500	Missouri	700-728	Railroad

- The middle two numbers are "group numbers," but many sets of these numbers have never been assigned. A social security number with an unassigned group number is automatically invalid.

- The Health and Human Services Administration issues notices of cancelled social security numbers to credit bureaus when a person dies. However, this system is extremely inefficient because it chiefly relies for reporting upon funeral homes, benefits paid to survivors, closed bank accounts, and even returned mail.

- Even if you do succeed in getting the Social Security Administration to assign you a new number (usually because of a religious objection), understand that the credit bureau computers will link your old number. A new, legitimate, social security number will not then give you a new identity.

- Remember, the fraudulent use of someone else's social security number violates the Social Security Act and the Justice Department will prosecute. Penalties range up to 5 years in prison or a fine of $50,000, or both.

3) *Feeding false information.* Here you contact the credit bureau where you have a negative report and advise them that there is incorrect information in the consumer identification section. It may be that the name or social security number is incorrect. You then give them new "correct" information which actually is false information. The credit bureau then "corrects" the file. Several weeks later you again contact the credit bureau and request a credit report. You then inform the credit bureau that none of the information is accurate, and the report must, in fact, belong to someone else with the same name.

The credit bureau will, of course, be obligated to verify the information. Since the information they must try to verify has nothing to do with the applicant, it can't be verified and the entire credit file must be deleted.

Finally, you wait several more months and again contact the credit bureau using your correct name, social security number etc., and instruct them to re-correct the information. They now return to their original credit report, but miraculously, it shows a clear credit history. What the bureau has done, of course, is to make their entire original credit report unverifiable, and in the process effectively wiped it clean to give you a new credit history.

You do not need these illegal scams to repair your credit. Follow only legal practices. It can achieve your goals easily without risking a criminal violation.

Key points to remember

- Lenders evaluate credit using the "three C's"—Capacity, Collateral and Character.

- Establish credit slowly but surely through secured bank loans and passbook loans.

- Always repay your loans early. It looks great on your credit report.

- Multiple loans multiply your creditworthiness.

- Secondary bankcards can automatically transfer someone else's good credit card history to your credit report.

- Secured bankcards are a surefire way to establish credit.

- Co-signers can help you establish credit regardless of how poor your credit may be.

- Never use fraudulent credit building strategies.

How To Protect Your Credit In Good Times And Bad

6

How To Protect Your Credit In Good Times And Bad

Sound financial planning is a key to maintaining your credit. Even during the hard times, your desire, willingness and ability to honor your obligations ensures it. But do you know the process for good financial planning; how to plan a budget, identify budget problems, and how to use and revise your budget? I will show you how in this chapter. We will also tackle and avoid those big problems that destroy credit: nonpayments, late payments, bankruptcy, foreclosure, repossession, and tax liens.

How to prepare your budget

Before you prepare your budget you must know the difference between a debt and an expense. A debt is any type bill you owe that can be permanently paid off. Examples are your car payment, credit cards, boat loan, dentist bills, and club fees. Conversely, rent, gas, electricity, phone bill, car insurance and groceries are on-going expenses that will likely be with you for the rest of your life.

List all of your debts. Include the current monthly payment, the balance and the projected payoff date. This will come in handy when you're ready to prepare your budget.

A well prepared budget begins your financial plan. Whether you plan a weekly, monthly or yearly budget, you must estimate your available income and allocate it to cover all your expenses within that period. Preparing a budget is the one most important step to financial stability. Your budget also measures how much money you will devote to each aspect of your life. Because your budget measures how your actual expenses match your desired expenses, the budget also is a guide to future spending, promptly paying your bills and maintaining your good credit.

Budget period

Choose a budget period: a week, a month, three months, a year. Not all bills are due monthly so have the time period closely coordinate expenses with income. Most families use a 12 month budget but you need not start your budget in January. You can start any time during the year. If this is your first budget, do a trial run using a shorter time frame to start.

For a yearly budget, divide your income and expenses by the number of your pay periods. Most people are paid weekly or bi-weekly. Most bills are paid monthly and not all are due at the same time each month. Estimate the due date of the bills and allocate your paychecks accordingly. Also allocate part of each paycheck towards new future expenses that you may foresee.

Budget preparation

Your paycheck stubs, tax returns, credit card bills, check books and other financial records will give you an accurate picture of where you stand today and also help you to prepare your budget. To obtain a clearer picture of your future expenditures, review your records to see your historical monthly expenditures. Confine your expenditures to your present living expenses. Do not include your debts for now.

Incomes and expenses will vary from month to month so use a separate budget for each month. Compare your monthly income and expenses as the difference between them will produce either a monthly surplus or deficit. This information is critical to anticipate cash shortages or a cash surplus.

Balance your budget

Now it's time to balance your budget. Compare your income with your expenses during the budget period. Are you satisfied with the outcome? Do you have any money left for emergencies? If your expenses exceed your income, review your plan again. What expenses can you eliminate? Where are you overspending? Decide what is most important and what can wait. Check flexible expenses when you want to trim expenditures. For example:

- Can you cancel book club memberships or magazine subscriptions?
- Must you belong to the country club?
- Is it vital to dine out every weekend?
- Can you survive without a house cleaning service?
- Can you live without a vacation this year?
- Is cable television absolutely essential?
- Must all your laundry go to the dry cleaners?

Once your flexible expenses are trimmed, reduce your fixed expenses. If rent takes a big chunk of your budget, why not move to more affordable housing until you are debt-free? Or extend your mortgage. How about your car payments? Are you driving more car than you can afford?

Less expensive transportation is an alternative that also can reduce your insurance costs. Have you reviewed your insurance lately? There is usually big savings there.

If you've made all possible expense reductions and your expenses still exceed your income, then consider other ways to increase your income. A higher paying job? A second job? Is your spouse employed? If not, why not become a dual-earner family or why not let your children earn their spending money by mowing grass or baby-sitting?

If your income exceeds your expenses, then congratulations! But don't buy something expensive simply because you have surplus cash. Instead, increase your savings to attain future goals, guard against emergencies, and build the financial stability everyone needs.

Reworking your budget

Revising your budget to correct financial problems requires both objectivity and detailed analysis. Only a solid, well-defined budget helps you to control your expenses and define your right spending level. Because a budget is determined by your current financial status, it must be flexible and respond to change. You may lose or change jobs, move or face an unexpected emergency that could wipe out your savings. When a significant financial event occurs, you should review your budget and make the necessary adjustments. In any case, you should review and revise your budget at least annually.

Your expenditures should never exceed 90% of your take home pay. The remaining 10% should be allocated to pay debts. Once you begin to pay these debts your accumulated extra cash can become your savings. Use your budget to prevent overspending, but allow yourself the freedom to reasonably spend more as your debts fall further behind you.

Encourage your family to participate in the budgeting process. Hold them accountable for their spending. Convene frequent family meetings to discuss what is really needed, versus what is wanted. Once you agree on the things that are truly needed, then narrow it to what you really want and can still afford. Is it a family vacation? A new car? New furniture? Shared family goals provide a greater incentive: It's much easier to forego a dinner and show, or new dress, when you know another more important dream moves closer to realization.

It's also important that one family member becomes responsible for financial planning. Two-income families often encounter problems when no one assumes responsibility for the overall plan. It doesn't matter who is in charge provided that someone is responsible for the overall plan. Finally, always keep accurate records, especially during the first year when you are trying to find a workable budget.

Use your savings to pay small debts

If you have more than three (preferably six) month's salary in your savings account, then consider using the surplus to pay off some of your smaller debts. But do not deplete your savings account. Maintain at least a three-month, but preferably six-months salary, for an emergency cushion just in case. When you consider the interest you earn in a savings account versus the interest you pay on credit cards, it makes sense to use this money to pay down those high-interest credit cards!

Yes, you can avoid bankruptcy

Now, let's tackle those serious credit-killers. No matter how depressed or deeply in debt you are, there are alternatives to bankruptcy for eliminating debt. Too many people mistakenly view bankruptcy as their only "way out." But, many who have filed bankruptcy have learned there is no one miracle formula for getting out of debt and bankruptcy may be the wrong formula.

Even when faced with threats of wage garnishment, auto repossession, or even foreclosure on your house, there are other lights at the end of the tunnel—alternatives to bankruptcy for solving your financial problems—without ruining your good credit Borrowing to raise cash, negotiating installment plans, and out-of-court settlements are three popular alternatives.

You can use one debt-reducing method or combine strategies into an overall program. How do you determine which method is best for you? First, determine your borrowing power. Add up your cash and what you can reasonably borrow. If this total exceeds your total debts, then a debt consolidation loan may be all you need.

Second, determine your income power. Divide your annual take-home pay (after deductions) by 12 to get your monthly take-home pay. Write down all non-monthly expenses (i.e., car insurance may come due only once a year), and divide that total by the number of months remaining until the end of the year. This gives you a monthly "save" amount to set aside for those bills when they come due.

Now list your monthly fixed expenses. Include your rent, gas, car or transportation costs, utilities, groceries, insurance, clothing, child care, child support, telephone, entertainment, etc. Add up all costs and subtract that total from your monthly take-home pay.

Next calculate your monthly variable expenses. These include all your debts, such as charge cards, bank loans, medical or dental bills, loans from relatives, etc. Subtract these monthly payments from your monthly take-home pay.

Is there any money remaining? If so, this is your cash-overflow, or disposable income that can be used to repay loans, credit cards and any other existing debts. If you have no money left, you will have to consider other debt reduction options—such as debt consolidation or creditor resolution agreements.

If your combined borrowing and income power allows you to fully pay off your overdue debts within one year, then you can probably solve your problems by reaching an agreement with creditors to extend your debt payments.

However, if you cannot resolve your past obligations within 12 months, then you may require an out-of-court settlement, a wage earners plan or even bankruptcy, as you probably cannot fully repay your creditors.

Borrowing to pay your debts

This may sound contradictory, but borrowing to pay your debts can be a sound way to stretch debt so that your monthly payments become more manageable. But this alternative is only if you are certain that borrowing will finally solve your debt problems. If you are seriously considering bankruptcy, then raising cash to pay your debts is foolish since bankruptcy will discharge your debts. Why waste your time on these alternatives if you are a serious bankruptcy candidate?

But if you are a good loan candidate, where do you turn? If you are lucky, your friends or relatives may help you with a loan. They are more likely to be supportive and less likely to require your home, car or other property as collateral. Their interest rates will also be lower.

Carefully explain your situation. Show whom you will pay with the loan proceeds. Present your future budget. Offer reasonable interest—even to friends and family. But before you do approach mom and dad or your best friend, consider these points:

- Can your parents really afford to help you or do they themselves scrimp by on their income? Is your friend raising five kids? Borrowing money from these people may be more of a hardship on them than they might willingly admit.

- Be sure you can handle the emotional strings that always attach to such the borrowed money. Will your father constantly remind you that you borrowed from him to pay your bills? Will your friend monitor how you spend your money? Can you take this scrutiny?

- Are you positive the borrowed money will get you out of debt once and for all or are you only delaying an inevitable bankruptcy?

- Can your parents or friends wait to have you repay the money when you are back on your feet and financially stable or must you start repayment immediately? If you must repay immediately, you may just be piling one more bill on to an already overburdened budget.

- Will your parents treat the loan as part of your eventual inheritance? If you will have one less bill to repay, you may just be able to get ahead of your bills once and for all.

Avoid the small army of unscrupulous lenders who are anxious to exploit people in financial difficulty. These lenders usually use misleading lending tactics, charge exorbitant interest rates, and collect "advance fees" for loans they never produce.

Some financial institutions advertise "debt consolidation, debt reorganization, or debt pooling" loans. Should you apply for this type loan, be prepared to pay exceptionally high interest and to pledge your home, car or other assets as collateral. Of course, it is not unusual, nor unreasonable, for the financial institution to require your home or car as security considering your financial picture.

Review the loan documents thoroughly. Read the fine print. Make sure you understand your obligations. Think it over carefully. Borrowing to consolidate your debts means that you have a longer pay back period and lower payments, but the interest you pay will be costly.

In addition to giving you the loan, some firms offer debt negotiations or negotiate settlements with your creditors. Raise caution flags when presented with this offer because these firms typically charge up to 35% of the amount you owe for this service.

Consumer finance companies grant consumers secured and unsecured loans. They usually require your home as collateral and charge from 15% - 18% interest on a loan that is really only a second mortgage on your home. Finance companies that make unsecured loans can charge about 25% for interest.

Borrowing against your assets is the easiest, fastest and most common way to raise the cash you need to pay your debts. Second mortgages, home equity loans, refinancing your home mortgage, or borrowing against a life insurance policy are all other possibilities.

Banks routinely issue second mortgages. They also refinance or arrange home equity loans. A home is the best collateral to use to secure a loan at lower interest. If you bought your home some years ago, the chances are good that you have equity in your home to borrow against.

Refinancing your home does put you back to square one on your goal to a free and clear home, but the equity in your home can lower your monthly payments on your excess obligations. Conversely, borrowing against your life insurance policy may leave you without coverage if the loan is not repaid.

Finally, you can borrow against your assets at a pawn shop. Do you have jewelry, electronics, mink coats, musical instruments, photography equipment, a coin collection, or anything else of value? A pawn shop will lend you about one-half the item's resale value and they give you several months to repay the loan before they resell your property.

Instead of borrowing against your assets you might sell some assets to pay your debts. It is best to sell an item with high resale value compared to its retail price. Quality artwork, stamp collections, electronics, book collections, and oriental rugs sell easily. Be objective when balancing personal wants against financial needs.

If you surrender a pledged item to a creditor (such as a car or washing machine) obtain a release because if the dealer doesn't sell the collateral for enough to cover your loan, he can sue you for a deficiency judgment. If you can't obtain a release from the dealer, then sell the item yourself. Even if you don't realize enough to fully pay the loan, you'll probably get more than the dealer who will only sell the item at auction.

There are many ways to sell assets for fast cash. Advertise in your local newspapers. Classifieds are a painless way to begin the process. Or advertise on bulletin boards at your local grocery store, church, work, post offices, schools or universities. Why not hold a yard sale, garage sale or auction?

Obviously, if you won't sell some property it will take you longer to pay your debts. And if you can't pay your debts, your creditors may ultimately take those items you won't sell willingly.

Communicate with your creditors

Never leave your creditors in the dark. Creditors hate when a customer pretends they never received past due notices or act indifferently when questioned about their overdue account.

When you have financial troubles, don't bury your head in the sand and pretend that your problems will go away. Your bills won't vanish unless you make them. Ignore your obligations and you force your creditor to collect through the courts. So communicate with your creditors. Once a creditor realizes that you have financial difficulties he may reduce your payments, extend the time to pay or make other reasonable adjustments to help you out. Creditors don't want to lose you as a customer—especially if they believe you are making a good faith effort to meet your obligations.

Write to your creditors or speak to them personally to explain your situation. Whether it's a temporary job loss or a more permanent problem, most creditors will work with you. But make your case. Tell them what actions you are taking to meet your bills. Do you plan to sell your house, borrow from your parents or consolidate your loans? Are you looking for a new job or will disability benefits begin soon? And if you have some money after you pay your essential expenses, try to send your creditors a token payment. Even a very small payment shows the creditor that you are making a good faith attempt to pay.

Negotiating an installment plan

Negotiating an installment plan with a creditor works when the creditor realizes that your only other option is a bankruptcy where the creditor will get even less. Creditors try to keep you from filing bankruptcy when that's in their best interest. But, if you have a steady income, there is no need to file for bankruptcy. Only threaten bankruptcy. Here are seven more negotiating tips for settling with creditors for pennies on the dollar.

1. *Be honest and up front with your creditors.* But paint that dark financial picture. Detail your hardships such as job layoffs, deaths in the family, serious medical problems, car repossessions, home foreclosures, etc.

2. *Tell the creditor your bottom line settlement offer and stick to it.* If you owe the dentist $1600 but can only pay $600 over six months — tell the dentist that and be firm. Don't offer more. Stick to that bottom line number. Even if you are not seriously considering bankruptcy...say you are!

3. *Never tell your creditors where you bank or work.* This is for your future protection. If the creditor obtains a judgment against you, it will be easier to collect if they know where you bank or work.

4. *If you make payments to your creditors*, use a money order purchased at a post office, convenience store or bank, other than your own.

5. ***Estimate the creditor's bottom line and push for a better deal.*** If you're three months behind in your car payment and the bank agrees to waive interest on two months, then push them to waive six months interest.

6. ***Don't believe a bill collector.*** If you negotiate with a bill collector who says he can only accept $100 on your account, don't believe it. Offer $50 as your bottom line figure. A bill collector must always check with their client and a client may accept your lower offer.

7. ***Bargain with cash.*** If a creditor will accept 50% of the total bill owed in installments, he may accept 30% in one lump sum payment. This is a better deal for you even if you must borrow the money to do it. You'll come out ahead in the long run. Money—not promises to pay—turn a creditor's head.

For any installment plan to work, you must convince most of your creditors to accept it. Give them the information they need. Submit a list of your debts, a budget and a proposed pay-back plan.

There are three types of installment plans. The first is self-administered where you contact your creditors directly.

The second is administered by a credit counselor. Creditors are more likely to accept your plan if it's handled this way because they know the credit counselor will make every possible effort to make you pay your debts.

The third is the Wage Earner's Plan which is a Bankruptcy Court-administered plan.

The self-administered creditor plan

Here you send a certified, return receipt requested, letter along with your budget and plan for repayment to each creditor. Have your letter explain your financial circumstances and request a reduction or moratorium of payments until your financial picture improves (see sample letters in the Appendix). Include your budget which should be simple, yet show how your money is spent. Consider how creditors look at your budget. They will be scrutinizing it to see that you made the necessary sacrifices. When you request a reduced payment, creditors will expect you to temporarily reduce your standard of living to show your sincerity.

How much should you offer? Subtract your living expenses from your monthly income. The difference is what is available for your creditors. Divide that amount proportionately between your creditors. Never favor one creditor. Exclude mortgages, car loans, taxes, and child support payments. These have priority over general creditors and must be fully paid.

The credit counselor administered plan

Credit counselors can help you set up your budget and will negotiate with your creditors. You can choose from three types of credit counselors.

Non-profit credit counselors negotiate a payment plan with all of your creditors. They do not charge fees but ask creditors for a donation (usually a 15% rebate) to cover their overhead and expenses. Most creditors quickly comply since they realize that without the counselor they probably wouldn't be paid at all. So, it's in the creditor's best interest to support the non-profit credit counselors. Caution: These agencies will force you to repay 100 percent of your debts even when that is unreasonable. Keep in mind that their allegiance is to the creditors—not you.

If you can afford it, a *for-profit bill paying service* will offer you a superior service. They ensure all your past due payments are brought current, and they make you adopt a very strict budget plan. After your bills are current, they ensure that future bills are paid timely. For-profit bill paying services also help you maintain your good credit rating and permit you to gradually expand your credit.

Forget the *pro-raters or debt poolers* who take a percentage of your income off the top. In most cases they do not first have your repayment plan approved by the creditors, and after they take their fee there is usually too little money left to satisfy your creditors. Your good intentions fall apart before you even present your plan to your creditors.

To locate a counseling agency in your area, contact:

- The National Foundation for Consumer Credit, 1819 H Street, Washington, DC 20006
- Your yellow pages under Consumer Credit Counselors
- Family Service America, 11700 W. Lake Park Drive, Milwaukee, WI 53224
- Your bank, credit union, department store or legal aid societies.

The Wage Earner's Plan

Never file a Wage Earner Plan (Chapter 13 Bankruptcy), or any other type bankruptcy, unless you first exhaust your other options. Bankruptcy should be an extreme last resort. But, if you do choose bankruptcy, consider the Wage Earner's Plan. It will least harm your credit.

The Wage Earner's Plan—(also known as filing Chapter 13)—is a form of bankruptcy where you usually repay all your debts to the extent you have assets, over three to five years.

With the Wage Earner's Plan you set up a court-approved plan to pay your debts. Once the court approves your repayment plan, a trustee is appointed to administer your case. Payments are usually deducted from your paycheck, and the trustee disperses these funds to your creditors monthly. If your payments are not made on time, your case can be dismissed. Creditors also can petition the court to increase payments if your financial situation improves.

Caution: Before you file any type bankruptcy, consult an attorney with expertise in bankruptcy law.

The seven big benefits of a wage-earners plan are:

- You are protected from foreclosure, repossession and eviction.

- Your credit report will not reflect subsequent "negative marks" from the non-payment of your debts—but the bankruptcy is reported.

- You will avoid harassing calls from creditors and collection agencies as bankruptcy stops creditors from harassing you. But even a written demand to stop can deter harassment.

- Your debts will be automatically frozen after you file and creditors cannot add interest or late charges to your account.

- Your creditors cannot garnish your wages.

- You can later re-establish your credit.

- You can keep all your property while you repay your obligations.

Remember, bankruptcy can be a powerful legal tool, but it is not always your wisest decision. Proceed cautiously. Weigh your options.

How to avoid foreclosure

If you miss your mortgage payments the lender that holds your loan can foreclose. A foreclosure is a credit killer on any credit report.

Banks and other lenders dislike foreclosure. It is time consuming, expensive and the property may sell for too little to cover your outstanding loan. So lenders will work with you if you are realistic.

Once you realize that you cannot pay on time, contact and negotiate with your lender before foreclosure begins. Try to work out the problem with these 12 solutions:

1. *Sell your house.* If you cannot afford the house, then sell it as quickly as possible to pay the loan. A sale is better than a foreclosure because it avoids both a negative entry on your credit report and costly attorney's fees. Most importantly it can preserve your equity because you get your best price through a voluntary sale.

2. ***Offer to make the lender your partner.*** If you can't afford the mortgage, the lender may accept part of the equity in the property, and in return, cancel part of the loan. This is a more likely solution if the property is quickly appreciating in value.

3. ***Equity-share with a third party.*** If the lender won't trade part of the loan for a share in the property, it may be an attractive investment to someone who will advance the funds to pay the mortgage.

4. ***Offer additional collateral.*** Offer additional collateral to ward off foreclosure. This works well when the loan value is close to the value of the property, and the lender believes he may take a loss through a forced sale. Additional collateral makes the lender more secure and he can then be more lenient.

5. ***Refinance.*** Do you have a short-term or high interest loan? Refinancing may substantially reduce your monthly mortgage payment. Calculate your new mortgage payment with a lower-interest, longer-term loan.

6. ***Secure a second mortgage.*** If you have equity in your property a second mortgage may be the answer. A second mortgage can bring the first mortgage current. This, however, is only a short term solution unless you can afford to pay both mortgages.

7. ***Borrow against other assets.*** If you can't obtain a second mortgage, perhaps you can borrow against some other asset to bring the mortgage current. Again, this requires you to pay an additional loan.

8. ***Offer interest only as a temporary solution.*** Occasionally a lender will accept interest only if you can show that your problem is temporary. This may reduce your mortgage payment considerably.

9. ***Offer a bonus.*** If you can't convince your lender to accept interest-only for a short time, then why not offer

a few "points" as a bonus? This is attractive to lenders— if the interest rate on the loan is lower than the prevailing rates.

10. *Negotiate a "hold" on payments.* If a lender believes there is adequate equity in your property, he may agree to a short-term moratorium on your payments. (interest and principal).

11. *Seek a co-signer.* If the lender questions the collateral value of your property, he may become more lenient if you add a creditworthy co-signer on the loan.

12. *Consider a Wage Earner's Plan/Chapter 13.* As discussed earlier, when all else fails you can file a Wage Earner's Plan (Chapter 13) to prevent foreclosure, although you must have to stay current on future payments. If your property is "over financed," the Wage Earner's Plan is an excellent way to reduce the loan to the actual value of the property.

How to stop repossession of your personal property

With a secured debt you pledge personal property or "collateral." If you default on your payments the lender can foreclose and sell the personal property you pledged as collateral for the loan. A default occurs if you miss even one payment. Read your security agreement carefully so you comply with all its terms. If you make timely payments but fail to comply with these other terms, you may still be in default and lose your property.

Refinancing is a popular option with auto loans. Finance companies prefer this. If they feel you can pay the new "low" monthly payment they will keep refinancing. But avoid the refinancing cycle. Use it only to bail yourself out in an emergency.

If you're past due on a bank loan and you have a checking or savings account with that bank, they can automatically collect the amount due from your account. Consider moving your funds to another bank.

As with other lenders, banks and finance companies hate to go to court to seize assets. Communicate with them. Show your willingness to make good on the loan and your eventual ability to do so. They then won't rush to seize or repossess your assets.

Auto sales are fueled by easy credit. This causes problems because people easily borrow when they cannot pay the loan. So banks and finance companies must have fast, effective collection procedures to aggressively collect on auto loans.

Most strategies used to avoid real estate foreclosures can equally succeed in preventing repossession of an auto, boat or other personal property. This is because both lender groups are in a similar position. So use the same negotiating techniques.

After a lender seizes your property he can sell it in any "commercially reasonable manner." The proceeds of the sale are then applied to the outstanding debt, costs of repossession and sale, and attorney's fees and legal expenses associated with the repossession and sale. The balance, if any, is returned to you. You remain liable for any deficiency.

Judgments and your credit

If you are sued and lose, the court will award the creditor a "judgment" against you. Credit bureaus or any interested party can obtain this information since it is public record. When a court awards a creditor a "money judgment," you are required to pay the dollar amount of the judgment.

Confession of Judgment

A "confession of judgment," in most states applies only to real estate contracts. If it is provided in your contract it automatically gives the creditor the right to a judgment against you if you do not fully pay the debt. The creditor need not go to court to get a judgment because you waived your right to a trial.

Deferred Judgments

Your creditor may agree to accept a "deferred judgment." Here you agree to pay a specific amount of money until the balance is fully paid. The lawsuit is then dismissed with no judgment ever entered against you. You must make the agreed payments or the creditor can petition the court to sign and enter the judgment.

Deficiency Judgments

If the lender succeeds in foreclosing on your property, the proceeds from the sale will be applied to the balance of the loan. Depending on your loan terms and your state laws, the lender may then get a "deficiency judgment" against you—if the proceeds do not cover the balance due on the loan. You will be held personally responsible for the difference between the sale proceeds of the property and the balance of the loan if you personally guarantee the debt. One way to avoid a deficiency judgment is to give the lender the property "in lieu" of foreclosure or repossession. This saves the lender the expense and delay of foreclosure and you can bargain for no adverse entry on your credit report.

A judgment against you and entered into the public records can remain on your credit report for seven years unless your state laws allow a longer time. Some states also allow a creditor to renew their judgment. To secure new credit you must then explain to a potential lender the circumstances surrounding the judgment.

Once a creditor has a judgment against you, your financial life is open to the creditor's prying eyes. Nothing is safe or secure. A judgment creditor will want to know the assets you own and where they are located in order to attach or seize them to satisfy the judgment. Your best option: Negotiate to settle before a lawsuit is even filed.

More creditor negotiation strategies

All negative marks on your credit report result from the credit reporting system. This system allows—even encourages—your creditors to report every negative credit transaction, from late payments to judgments. But if you can gain your creditor's cooperation you can keep those negative entries off your credit report. You gain a creditor's cooperation through negotiation. Your goal is to persuade creditors to either tone down or entirely delete their remarks on your credit report.

Negotiating is bargaining. Each side offers something the other wants. Your job is to offer your creditor what he most wants. What do creditors want? The money you owe them, or as much of it as possible. By negotiating repayment plans you must sincerely demonstrate your ability to make regular payments on time, pay off the debts you owe, and revive their interest in you as a customer. You must trade money for a positive credit rating on your credit report or alternatively, get the creditor to agree not to report a negative credit transaction. Here's how:

1. *Make a "win-win" offer to the creditor.* This is your most effective offer. Often, a creditor has no expectation of full payment. Offer a payment schedule in exchange for a promise to improve your payment history and you may find your creditor only too willing to deal. For example, you may agree to pay 100 percent of the debt in 12 monthly installments if the creditor agrees to recognize your new bill-paying commitment with a better credit rating. Be specific when you deal with a creditor. Or perhaps the creditor may agree to withhold a negative report as long as you pay in a timely manner, or he may raise your credit rating after six months of prompt payment on a settlement. You see the idea!

2. **Obtain "open account" status.** It looks bad when your account is closed to further purchases when you are making regular payments. So when negotiating an offer with your creditor, ask him to reopen your account while you uphold your end of the bargain. You can be most persuasive when you offer to pay 100 percent of the debt, perhaps with some added incentive such as a service charge or interest. This extra effort is certainly worth it if your creditor allows you to keep your credit or agrees not to further damage it. But be certain that

whatever terms you finally agree upon are within your budget so you do faithfully keep your promise.

3. *Put it in writing.* Once you have reached a verbal agreement with your creditor, it is vital to put it in writing. Type up a letter listing all the points of agreement and send it to the creditor with a stamped, self-addressed envelope. Once your creditor signs the agreement and returns it to you, it can become part of your credit record.

4. *Honor the agreement.* Be responsible! Now that you have a written agreement, you need only fulfill it and your credit rating will be saved. You must be punctual! Not only must every payment be made on time, you should make your payments ahead of time, if possible. If your ability to meet the payment schedule in the agreement becomes threatened by unemployment or illness, then inform your creditor immediately and before you miss any payments. Explore mutually satisfactory ways to solve your temporary setback. This is the key to preserving your credit.

Key points to remember

- Sound financial planning is vital to maintaining good credit.

- Sound financial planning begins with a realistic budget—one that allows you to live comfortably within your means.

- Trim your budget by first trimming flexible expenses. Then rework your fixed expenses.

- Your objective is a budget where your income exceeds your expenses.

- Never write bad checks.

- Use debt reduction, creditor negotiation and cash raising strategies to avoid loan defaults.

- Avoid the five credit killers: bankruptcy, judgements, foreclosure, repossession, and tax seizures.

Credit Card
Secrets

Credit Card Secrets

For most people, good credit means the ability to obtain credit cards—such as Visa and MasterCard—so they can again charge their day-to-day purchases.

But here's a big secret: You can get a credit card without good credit or a high income. Yet few people know how. Most people follow incorrect procedures, get turned down, and wrongly conclude that they cannot qualify for a Visa or MasterCard.

Many people with good credit histories and high incomes also get turned down for credit cards, while less creditworthy people carry a pocketful of credit cards. How *do* they do it?

The credit card world can be simple to navigate when you understand its rules. But to the uninformed it is indeed mysterious.

An inside look at the credit card system

You don't need dozens of credit cards. Smart use of your credit cards is important, not how many cards you possess. If there are advantages to possessing many credit cards, it is in their proper use, not their dollars of potential credit. But to get those valuable credit cards you must first know the secrets of the credit card system.

Once you understand how banks cooperate with each other you will understand how to deal with the credit card companies. Banks do work closely to track their cardholders, and most banks want to know how many credit cards you now have before they issue one of their own.

Banks share a computer to trade this vital cardholder information. When a bank discovers you have too many cards (each bank has their own policy on how many cards are "too many"), they automatically reject your application. Banks that offer the same card usually disallow repeat cards to a cardholder. You may obtain only one card from an interconnected network of cooperating banks.

How does a bank card system actually work?. When you apply for a credit card at your local bank, many events occur. While your local bank's name is proudly displayed on your credit card, odds are that your card was instead issued by a different bank.

Interconnected banks trade favors and reciprocate functions. Banks also hire each other to perform different services to economize.

Most consumers are unaware of this interbank arrangement. But when you apply for a bank credit card, the bank must perform many functions which the bank normally cannot afford to do on its own. The bank then seeks the assistance of other banks.

Bank card systems are complicated. First, they must accept the new applications, obtain credit reports and establish approved accounts. Then the actual cards must be printed and embossed. Ongoing paperwork includes endless statements, sales brochures, late payment notices and countless other details that make a credit card program succeed.

Few banks can undertake every function required to operate a credit card program. So to avoid this complicated and costly process, some banks act as credit card agents for others. Usually the smaller banks contract with the larger banks who chiefly perform card-related services. But many different service packages are available. The largest card processing centers usually handle accounting, credit checks, mailings, statements, collections and administrative details for the small banks. The smaller bank pays as a fee a percentage of its annual credit volume.

Both the large and small banks benefit from this relationship. However, many smaller banks are now establishing their own computer systems to reap the big profits generated from operating their own large credit card processing center.

This bank card system allows the smaller bank to "stay in the credit card game." This saves the small bank the expense of costly computers and additional personnel. With today's fierce interbank competition, both large and small banks must offer the credit cards that are important to bank promotion and serve as a major advertising tool to attract new customers.

Larger banks benefit from this service arrangement because their overhead becomes partially subsidized from the annual service fees they receive from the smaller institutions that use their card center services. Some card processing centers earn handsome profits.

Bank networks commonly sub-divide parts of the credit card process. One bank may offer the card, another may handle credit checks, a third (or fourth) bank the embossing and monthly statement function. Some "chains" may be short, others surprisingly long. Major banks may have many lines of agent banks stretching in a lengthy chain. Other chains may encompass only three or four agent banks. What then happens if you simultaneously apply for credit cards from several local banks? Although you may apply to different banks, many will be connected to the same major bank. This, of course, raises two possibilities:

1) The major bank will have a relationship with the agent banks that prevents the applicant from obtaining more than one card from the major bank. Apply to twelve banks connected to the same major bank and the major bank will only issue one card.

Duplicate credit card accounts are seldom allowed. With several applications from the same individual processed by a major bank, the first application accepted becomes your account. All others are automatically cancelled as they enter the central computerized system. Your credit card will then bear the name of the accepting bank. But in the process you generated potentially harmful inquiries on your credit report.

2) A major bank will issue several cards to the same individual if the agent bank assumes responsibility for your credit. The agent bank would then assume responsibility for any default in payment.

Uncovering those chains that issue duplicate cards requires detective work, but it is worth the effort if your objective is to own multiple bank credit cards.

Types of credit cards

There are three types of credit cards. Each has its own special use and credit characteristics.

1) **Bank cards (Visa, MasterCard)**. Issued only by banks, savings and loans, and credit unions. The bank cards (MasterCard and Visa) give merchants the opportunity to sell on credit. The banks pay the merchant, less a nominal 1 to 4 percent service charge. The advantages to the merchant? No accounts receivable (no credit risk or credit and collection costs), and higher sales because customers can buy on credit.

Each issuing bank sets its own credit policies (fees, credit criteria, credit limits, interest rates, billings). Visa and MasterCard issue no cards, but serve only as a clearinghouse. Credit transactions (adjustments and credit disputes) remain between the customer and issuing bank.

2) **Travel and entertainment cards (American Express, Diner's Club, Carte Blanche)**. American Express is the clear leader. "T&E" cards are not exclusively used for travel and entertainment. Virtually any consumer items or service can be obtained with these cards. American Express, for instance, competes

aggressively with the bank cards for retail credit purchases—although retailers prefer the bank cards because they charge the retailer a smaller service fee.

"T&E" cards charge an annual fee of about $50 (to $300 for the prestigious American Express Platinum Card) and also require full payment each month. Bank cards, on the other hand, encourage installment payments so they can earn interest.

Because there is only one source for each T&E card, they are considerably more difficult to get than bank cards. Moreover, T&E card companies tolerate late payments less and will quickly revoke credit at the first sign of financial difficulty.

3) **Merchant or "affinity" credit cards**. This is the oldest type of credit card and it only involves the merchant and customer. Issued by department stores, chains, oil companies, airlines, car rental agencies and similar sellers of goods and services, they seldom charge an annual fee and like bank cards, usually encourage extended payments both to spur buying and to earn interest.

Is your credit card a good deal?

Most consumers are surprised to discover the many available choices when selecting a bank credit card. Examine your options carefully before selecting your credit card!

Credit cards are not the same. And don't believe you must live in the bank's state or have an account to get a bank's credit card.

There are some great credit card bargains. There are also plenty of cards to avoid. So carefully compare bank policies before you select your cards. Review these four bank card features:

1) **Transaction fees.** Banks know that about half their cardholders completely pay their total balance each month to limit their service fees. So to compensate and increase revenue some banks impose transaction fees.

For example, a major California bank charges 12 cents each time the card is used. Cardholders convinced the $10 annual fee was a bargain were less aware of the expensive transaction fees. But people who frequently use these cards find their transaction fees add up quickly. So check transaction fees. Cards that require no transaction fees are usually far less costly than those with transaction fees.

2) **Annual membership fees.** Annual fees boost sagging credit card income for the banks. Because most people fully pay their monthly statements to avoid finance charges, banks find annual fees are vital for their survival. But some banks will waive their annual fees if you keep a minimum balance in your checking account. Intelligently evaluate the real value of this offer. See what the interest rate would be for the average amount on deposit. Low interest means lost income—income that could be earned from another bank that pays higher interest. The lost interest may even exceed what you save through free annual membership.

3) **Finance charges/annual percentage rate (APR).** Credit card interest rates vary between 9 percent and 22 percent, although each state sets a legal limit. For instance, the District of Columbia limits interest rates to 18 percent (and disallows annual fees).

Many banks don't state their annual percentage rates on their applications because their interest rates frequently change with the fluctuating interest rate indicators, and the interest charged by competitors. You then won't know the actual interest rate until the credit card arrives and you sign the credit card agreement. Since a card in the hand is worth two in the bush, the new cardholder seldom musters the willpower to return a new credit card—even when it carries a high interest rate.

Always check how interest is calculated. A bank may calculate interest three ways:

a) *Average daily balance*-This most popular method is calculated by taking the previous billing balance and subtracting any payment received. The finance charge is then calculated on that amount.

b) *Adjusted balance*-This least expensive method calculates the finance charge levied against the remaining balance. Purchases during the month are not charged interest until the following month.

c) *Previous balance*-The finance charge is on the balance at the beginning of the month, without considering prior payments until the following month.

The Truth in Lending Act requires all credit cards to disclose their method of finance charge and the annual true percentage rate (APR).

Credit card finance charges are high. So fully pay your credit card each month. Under the Tax Reform Act of 1986, credit card interest is no longer deductible.

4) **Credit limit.** Credit limits also can vary considerably between bank cards. One bank may set a $1,000 credit limit, another $2,000. Some banks are quite lenient on credit, others are stringent. Banks consider several factors when establishing a credit limit. Most important is your credit rating. Other factors include corporate policy, competition, funds availability and the economy. Be a discriminating credit card shopper. Find the best deals.

List the information supplied on your credit card application. Some of the information you need may not be contained in the application, however, you will want to know:

- What are the finance charges?
- What is the annual fee?
- What is the policy on cash advances?
- Are there restrictions on how you may use the card?
- Is there a grace period before finance charges begin?
- Does the bank compute finance charges by the adjusted balance method, the previous balance method, or the average daily balance method?

- Does the bank originate its own card or does another institution originate the card?
- Does the bank offer special services—such as "prestige cards" or automatic teller machines (ATMs)?
- What are the bank's collection practices, and how lenient are they with borrower "problems"?
- What is their credit limit?
- What are their minimum monthly payments?

Three more credit card features to look for

The credit card field is rapidly changing. Here are three relatively new features you should know about:

1) Automated teller machines (ATMs). Plastic cards are issued by banks for use in automatic machines. You receive a personal identification number (PIN) with each card. Each card has a magnetic strip which is activated when you punch in your PIN.

Originally designed only as cash dispensing cards, they now perform many functions: Deposits and withdrawals, cash advances on charge cards, bank transfers, account inquiries and even bill payments.

Although very convenient, ATM plastic does not offer the same protection you enjoy with regular credit cards. For example, if you report a stolen ATM card within two days of the theft, you have only a maximum liability of $50. However, if the theft goes unreported, you may be responsible for up to $500 on any loss.

Unauthorized withdrawals must be reported within 60 days of their initial appearance on the bank statement or your liability is unlimited. You could then lose your entire deposit. When handling an ATM account, always keep your PIN and ATM card separate.

2) Debit cards. The debit card is like the ATM card. Both cards are merely electronic replacements for a check. They are not an extension of credit.

3) Card enhancement features. This plan offered by Visa, MasterCard, and Prudential Securities for its Command Account, provides price protection when an item you purchase with these cards is later advertised at a lower price. You are reimbursed for a percentage of the difference in price. For example, Citibank reimburses its credit card users up to $150 per purchase with a maximum annual reimbursement of $1000. Prudential reimburses a maximum of $250 with an annual cap at $1000.

The ATM electronically draws cash in the same way a check can. The debit card also replaces a check by paying bills and making purchases via an electronic entry in your account. Bankers prefer debit cards over checks because check processing is generally less profitable.

To the extent debit cards replace credit cards, bankers will lose finance charges they normally collect.

Merchants prefer the debit card system because they get their money immediately, as it is electronically transferred into their company account (and safe from hold-ups). This electronic system means minimum paperwork. The merchant also has no worry about a check being misplaced or lost.

No one debit system operates nationwide because merchants and banks have yet to agree on a standardized system.

This process is not yet completely electronic. Debit card users still have to complete paperwork similar to a sales slip or MasterCard transcript when making a purchase. These slips are forwarded to the cardholder's bank, or a third party processor who agreed to handle debit accounts, and then deducted from the cardholder's account as normal checks are handled.

Because the debit card concept is new, some states have no laws that define the cardholder's liability in the event of unauthorized use or theft. Consult with the institution issuing a debit card to establish your liability.

3) Card enhancement features. This plan offered by Visa, MasterCard and Prudential Securities for its Command Account, provides price protection when an item you purchase with these cards is later advertised at a lower price. You are reimbursed for a percentage of the difference in price. For example, Citibank reimburses its credit card users up to $150 per purchase with a maximum annual reimbursement of $1000. Prudential reimburses a maximum of $250 with an annual cap at $1000.

10 surefire tips for obtaining credit cards

How do you get the credit cards you want? Here's ten tips:

1) List the banks from whom you will request applications. It may be easier to get credit cards from banks in your own state. The large national banks are generally most aggressive in accepting new accounts. But don't overlook savings and loan companies or credit unions. They also are good credit card sources. Another way to find aggressive banks? Solicit the help of friends or relatives with good credit. People with good credit are showered with credit card requests. Also check with your professional, trade or civic associations who sponsor a group bank card plan. You may find it easier to obtain a credit card as a member of the group.

2) Request an application form. When you write for a credit card application, do not send a form or computer-generated letter. Ask about finance charges and fees because these points often are not included on the application, and you will need this information to evaluate the bank's credit card policies. If you need more information about the bank's underwriting requirements, then meet personally with the loan officer.

3) Obtain your credit report from all credit bureaus used by the credit card issuer. If you have a negative credit report, then follow the earlier procedures to remove derogatory credit marks.

Applying for credit with negative marks on your report only invites refusal. So try to remove those negative marks *before* you submit your credit application.

If your credit report is less than positive, try to persuade your creditors to report positive credit information about you to the credit bureau. While the credit bureau can charge a fee for entering these reports, it is a worthwhile expense if it improves your credit standing.

Also check your debt to income ratio. Banks will seldom extend you credit if your fixed monthly obligations exceed 50 percent of your net income.

Some credit bureaus may not have negative reports on you. If such a credit bureau is used by your institution, you may succeed even with a poor credit report elsewhere. Large credit issuers generally subscribe to all three credit reporting agencies, but a smaller card issuer may not.

4) Don't simultaneously apply to card issuers that use the same credit bureau. Avoid multiple applications to credit card issuers who use the same credit bureau. You will then not be turned down because of too many inquiries.

Most credit card issuers automatically request your credit report from all three major credit bureaus when they receive your application. This inquiry will then appear on future credit reports. Remember: More than a few inquiries within a short period will hurt your credit.

5) Start with merchant credit cards. Department store cards, gas company cards and other retail credit cards are usually easier to obtain than bank credit cards. Check whether your payments on these company cards are reported to the credit bureau. Sometimes they are not. But if you punctually repay these cards it will boost your credit record and help you win bank credit cards.

Your payments on these merchants accounts may not be reported to a credit bureau. However, credit applications will ask about your other credit card accounts. A good payment record on more easily-obtained merchant accounts can give you the foundation to build more credit.

6) Let your bank loan officer help you to get a credit card. Ask your bank loan officer about a Visa or MasterCard. He will let you know whether you qualify for a card at his institution.

Also ask the bank official about your chances elsewhere. Different institutions have different policies, and your banker is likely to know the more lenient banks.

Your banker, in fact, may on his own recommend that you apply at another more lenient institution. Lending institutions with lower interest will tighten their credit to reduce losses. Conversely, banks with higher rates usually are more lenient with credit.

7) Review the terms of the various credit cards. Compare the various terms of credit cards available to you. But first decide which terms are most important to you.

For example, if your credit cards will finance expensive consumer purchases then you want a low annual interest. Will you use the card for daily purchases and fully pay each month to avoid finance charges? Then a no annual fee card with a long grace period is most advantageous.

The ideal card has no annual fee, low APR, a long grace period, and no surcharges. However, banks are in the business to make money, so no credit card features all these advantages.

8) Accurately complete your application. Complete as much information as possible on your bankcard credit application. Write neatly (type if possible). List at least one checking and savings account on your credit card application, even those with small balances. It is important to have a telephone in your name.

9) Request limited credit. If this is your first card (or if you had credit problems) then request limited credit. A bank may deny you $1,000 but give you a $500 credit line. But if you apply for $1,000, the bank may simply refuse your application and never suggest a $500 credit line. Once you have a credit card, you can always increase your limit by proving your creditworthiness.

10) Be persistent. If you are refused a credit card, the credit card company must tell you why. You can then correct or repair your credit as discussed in earlier chapters. You can also ask the credit card issuer how you can become an acceptable risk. A smaller credit line? More income? Correcting some credit problems? A co-signer? Communicate! If the bank still refuses, try another bank. Be persistent!

Avoid multiple credit card scams

Self-proclaimed finance experts advise you to acquire dozens—even hundreds—of bank cards. The reason for accumulating these cards is to build a huge unsecured credit line so you can invest in a wide number of schemes. For instance, 30 bank cards, each with a credit line of $1,000, puts $30,000 at your disposal. To accomplish this, you maintain a zero-balance on each account so you can legally avoid disclosing your other cards when you apply for additional cards. You then simultaneously draw down your credit on all accounts.

There are several obvious problems with this scheme. First, it may be fraudulent not to disclose your other cards, even if they have zero balances. Second, it is highly unlikely that you will find an investment that will give you the fast return needed to repay the cards. When you do fail to pay—as you inevitably will—you have 30 negative marks on you credit and can lose your credit for many years to come. Remember, credit cards are for convenience, not get-rich-quick schemes.

The secured credit card alternative

If you can't obtain an unsecured bank credit card, don't give up hope. Even with terrible credit or low income you *can* get a credit card. These credit cards are secured with collateral and are called "secured credit cards."

Why secured credit cards? Because lenders want to extend credit to make money. But they make money only if you repay. When you pledge collateral to secure the credit, the bank knows that one way or another they will get repaid. Banks are strict and loan officers rarely approve questionable loans. If your income is low, or you have poor, or no credit, then you will probably not get an unsecured credit card. But you may still qualify for a secured card. Or when you have borderline credit that qualifies you only for limited unsecured credit, you will get more credit if you pledge collateral to ensure payment.

The most popular collateral is, of course, a savings account at the bank that issues the card. This account secures the credit line on the credit card and cannot be used by the cardholder unless he surrenders the card or the card is exchanged for an unsecured card.

Sometimes the bank will let you hold your deposit in a CD or money market account. For example, a minimum deposit of $500 may be required to get the secured card and the credit line may be only half this amount, or $250. You will probably be charged an annual fee for the card. However, interest may be lower than industry average, because the credit is backed by collateral. Some institutions also charge an additional processing fee of about $50, which is usually refundable if the card is not approved. Other forms of collateral acceptable to a bank may include stocks, bonds, or an automobile or boat.

If you cannot get a secured credit card on the strength of your collateral, then try to obtain a card by recruiting a creditworthy co-signer. A friend or relative may co-sign, or you may offer payment for assuming the risk. The co-signer guarantees to make good on any obligations you incur. It's like sharing a card with the co-signer. The co-signer's credit supports yours, since yours alone can't support credit. A co-signer assumes a big responsibility. Don't ask someone to co-sign for you if you can't fulfill your obligations.

Are you are a student who can't obtain a credit card? Perhaps your parents will include you on their account until you can qualify for your own. Some credit cards even offer special deals to graduating seniors as a way to welcome them to the credit world.

Secured credit cards look exactly like unsecured bank cards. Only you and the bank will know the card is secured.

Because secured bank cards are backed with a cash deposit, the bank cannot lose. That is why they accept poor credit risks. But the secured credit line can give you the convenience of a credit card when you otherwise cannot obtain one. Equally important, once you prove your creditworthiness with a secured credit card, you can begin to build the credit you need for unsecured credit.

With a good track record on a secured bank card, the lender may issue you an unsecured bank card in place of the secured card. This is known as a conversion feature. Why would the institution swap a collateralized account for one that is unsecured? Since your unsecured card will offer higher credit, the bank believes you will use it more often and build higher monthly credit balances, providing for the bank higher interest, higher finance charges and more transaction fees.

Do you have some capital, but poor credit? You may consider a "debit" card as another type of secured credit card.

Debit cards also look like ordinary Visas or MasterCards. When you use them, you do not receive credit, but the bank charges one of your accounts in which you have funds. The debit card allows you the convenience of a credit card while allowing you to keep your funds at a higher interest money market account. Debit accounts are used like checking accounts. The big difference? It is easier to use a charge card than write a check, and some places accept charge cards but not checks.

If you have significant assets, but still cannot qualify for a credit card, then a debit card may be for you. Large brokerage firms, like Prudential Bache can set you up with a debit card if you open a money market account with them.

Don't forget, your good track record with a secured or debit card is not always reported to the credit bureau. Make it a priority to find those card issuers that do report your secured credit card history to a credit bureau. And request that they do. Your possession and responsible use of these cards creates valuable references for future use.

Cautions abound with secured or debit cards. For instance, you may have seen ads in national magazines or TV that guarantee Visa, MasterCard or other credit cards—even if you have poor credit. These companies, in most cases, merely take advantage of what you do not know: They only issue secured credit cards. They usually collect a "non-refundable" processing fee to merely send the customer a secured credit card application. Others only send a booklet or instructional sheet that explains "secured credit cards." Save the $25 to $50 these firms charge. With the information in this chapter, you can obtain credit cards on your own.

Where can you get a secured credit card? Check with your bank first. Many banks offer these cards, and your own bank will be most lenient with you because they already have a banking relationship with you. Explain that you want a secured account because you realize that you may not satisfy their credit requirements. This approach often works even if the bank is not actively seeking applications for secured cards. But do not be discouraged if your bank does not offer secured credit cards.

Walk through the telephone book. Call the credit card departments of the savings and loans. You may be lucky and find one located in your area—but remember, you do not need a local bank for an unsecured credit card. Issuing banks are scattered nationwide, and your transactions can be easily handled by mail, including billings, deposits and withdrawals. Also check these banks for secured credit cards:

American National Bank
1890 Palmer Ave., Ste. 403
Larchmont, NY 10538
(914) 833-0560

American Pacific Bank
P.O. Box 19360A
Portland, Oregon 97280-9360
(800) 879-8757
(800) 879-8745

Bank of Hoven
Credit Card Division
P.O. Box 9068
Van Nuys, California 91499-4009
(800) 777-7735

Bank One, Lafayette, NA
Credit Card Services
P.O. Box 450
Lafayette, IN 47902-0450
(800) 395-2556
(800) 395-2555

Budget and Credit Counseling Services, Inc.
Secured Card Program
115 East 23 ST. 11th floor
New York, NY 10010
(212) 505-2420
(212) 677-3066

Butterfield Savings and Loan
568 E. Lambert Rd.
Berea, California 92621
(800)828-6602
(800) 521-4748 (in California)

Central National Bank of Matoon
Secured Credit Card Program
Broadway and Charleston Avenue
Matoon, IL 619838
(800) 876-9119

Charter Savings Bank
Secured VISA Program
324 East First Street
Los Angelos, CA 9012
(213) 624-7434

Citibank
Citicorp Credit Services
P.O Box 7001
Hagerstowen, MD 21742
(800) 743-1332

Citibank South Dakota, NA
Treasury Dept. 1247
P.O. Box 6218
Sioux Falls, SD 57117-9783
(800) 743-1332

Citicorp Savings of Illinois
P.O. Box 87581
Chicago, Illinois 60680
(312) 997-5720

Community Bank of Parker
Spirit VISA
19590 East Main ST,
Parker, CO 80134-9900
(800) 770-8472

Continental Savings of America
Secured VISA
2895 Diamond Street
San Francisco, CA 94131
(415) 239-4500

Dreyfus Thrift & Commerce
P.O. Box 6003
Garden City, NY 11530-9841

Farrington Bank
U.S. Liberty, Inc.
P.O. Box 3320
Cherry Hill, NJ 08034-0440
(609) 488-6206

Fifth Third Bank
38 Fountain Square Plaza
Cincinnati, OH 45263
(800) 972-3030

First Consumers National Bank
Secured Loan Program
P.O. Box 2088
Portland, OR 97208-2088
(800) 876-3262

First Interstate Bank of South Dakota
Centennial Bankcard
125 Armstrong Road
Des Moines, IL 60019-9302
(800) 825-1158
(718) 515-0817

First Mutual Savings Bank
Secured VISA Program
P.O. box 1647
Bellevue, WA 98009
(206) 455-7808

First National Bank in
Brookings
700 22nd Avenue South
P.O. Box 784
Brookings, SD 57006-2680
(605) 692-2680

First National Bank of Marin
The Bankcard Service Center
P.O. Box 3696
San Clemente, CA 92674
(714) 498-2621

First State Bank
P.O. Box 15414
Wilmington, DE 19885-9394
(302) 322-4305

First Trade Union Savings
Bank
Secured Credit Card
Program
10 Drydock AVE.
P.O. Box 9063
Boston, MA 02205-9063
(800) 242-0273
(617) 482-4000

Key Federal Savings
210 Fifth Avenue
New York, NY 10010
(718) 768-6803

Key Federal Savings Bank
626 Revolution Street
P.O. Box 6057
Havre de Grace, MD 21078
(800) 228-2230
(301) 939-0016

New Era Bank
New Era Credit Card Center
675 Franklin Boulevard
P.O. Box 1369
Sommerset, NJ 08875
(908) 937-4600

Pioneer Federal Savings
Bank
Secured VISA Program
P.O. Box M
Lynwood, WA 98046
(206) 771-2525

Signet Bank
Card Center
P.O. Box C32131
Richmond, VA 23286-8873
(800) 333-7116

State Street Bank and Trust
Secured Credit Card Plan
P.O. Box 1899
Boston, MA 02105
(617) 654-4111

Texas Bank, NA
1845 Precinct Line Road
Hurst, TX 76054
(800) 451-0273

United Federal Savings
498 Clement Street
San Francisco, CA 94118

United Savings Bank
Secured Card Program
711 Van Ness Avenue
San Francisco, CA 94102
(415)929-6084

Key points to remember

- How you use credit is more important than the amount of credit you have.

- To avoid duplicate credit card applications, first determine which bank chains or links issue duplicate cards.

- Travel and entertainment cards are the most difficult credit cards to obtain because each card has only one source.

- Credit cards are either secured or unsecured. Secured cards are easier to obtain because they are backed by collateral.

- Shop the credit cards. Compare transaction fees, annual membership fees, finance charges, APRs, and credit limits.

- ATM and debit cards are not true credit cards because they offer no credit. They simply replace checks.

- Try to persuade creditors to report your positive credit transactions to the credit bureaus.

- Avoid multiple card scams.

- Ignore ads for credit cards in magazines or on TV from companies that guarantee a credit card.

How To Get Credit For The Essentials In Your Life

8

How To Get Credit For The Essentials In Your Life

Transportation and shelter: Life's two most essential needs. Because they are usually your two most expensive purchases, you will need good credit to obtain them. Do you dream of a new car? Owning your own home? Stop dreaming! Instead study and apply the techniques in this chapter. You will soon lease or buy that new car and you will find a mortgage for that new, beautiful home.

Financing your car

Despite poor credit or no credit, there *are* ways to finance good transportation. Say goodbye to buying a broken down heap for cash. A vehicle you can proudly drive can be in your future—with little or no cash down and little or no credit.

How? Let's assume you do want that new car. As you would expect, traditional financiers—banks and credit unions—primarily lend to those with good credit. Low-interest banks are most strict.

Credit unions generally are more lenient with car-loan credit. If you belong to a credit union, then candidly explain to them why you have problems on your credit report. Credit unions are as interested in your current financial situation as your past problems. Character and good faith more influence credit unions than they do banks. But both lender groups require a substantial deposit—up to 25 percent of the price of the car. If you can afford this high deposit and show sufficient income to make the payments, you should, even with shaky credit be able to finance a new car loan from a credit union.

If you are consistently turned down by banks *and* credit unions, then try the new car dealership. But not just any dealership. Select the largest dealership in your area. There is where you stand the best chance of financing your new car. Why? Understand how finance companies work with affiliated car dealerships. All car manufacturers operate their own finance or credit companies. They exist to help car dealerships sell more cars—and sell them faster. A dealer who can offer instant financing through the manufacturer's finance company obviously has a greater chance to make the sale because you never need to leave the showroom. Many different financing arrangements are available to dealers, so any customer with no credit history has a good chance for auto financing.

Larger dealerships provide their finance companies spectacular profits and these dealerships receive preferred treatment. This includes approval of more questionable loans. You won't necessarily be approved for a Rolls Royce, but the more your car matches what you can afford, the stronger your chances for financing.

Before you select your car, sit down with the salesman or credit manager to check the necessary down payment and the interest rate that will be charged. These two items are set by the finance company and are largely based upon your credit rating. The finance company advises the credit manager of its minimum terms, but some dealerships charge higher rates and pocket the difference. That's why you must negotiate rock bottom terms: price of the car, interest rate *and* down payment. If you already tried a bank or credit union you gained valuable experience— even if you were rejected. You know the prevailing interest rates. Remember, the dealership is in business to sell or lease cars and they are much more experienced with poor credit applicants than are traditional lenders. With poor credit you may not leave the dealership with a great bargain, but you may still find a car that satisfies your needs on terms you can afford.

One borrowing technique that works equally well with car dealerships and lenders is to find a co-signer for your loan. A co-signer pledges his good credit to get you the loan. No lender objects to your poor credit if your co-signer's credit is strong. However, you risk the co-signer's good credit. Reduce that risk. Buy term life insurance to cover the loan. But this only protects the co-signer if you die. A larger downpayment and paying your installments through your co-signer are two important safeguards for your co-signer.

A cosigner alternative is a straw-man sale. Here someone purchases the car in his own name and resells or leases it to you— usually at a good profit. But since you pay the straw man, this won't help you build your credit because your prompt payments will not appear on your credit report unless submitted by the strawman.

Another strategy is to structure a recourse loan with a larger dealership. Here, the dealership co-signs the loan to a bank. If you default, the bank has recourse to the dealership which then assumes the loan and repossesses the car. This arrangement usually requires a higher interest loan and larger down payment.

A still more useful financing technique with used cars and very poor credit is called *Buy-Here, Pay-Here*. Because used cars cost less than new ones, the dealer can more easily finance the car's full price. Your down payment may cover the dealer's entire cost. Your future payments then become the dealer profit. This financing is most common with older, low-priced cars, but some dealers sell late model cars this way. The problem? You will pay the dealer considerably more than what he paid for the car. And if you default on the payments the car is repossessed and resold.

Even with the most attractive financing, every used car must be carefully inspected by a mechanic. Before buying a used car, also check the car's actual worth by consulting the Blue Book, a guide that banks and car dealers use to determine a vehicle's wholesale value. Banks can also give you this information. Know approximately how much a *Buy-Here, Pay-Here* dealer paid for the car *before* you negotiate!

A final caution: Never buy credit life insurance from a car dealer. This is *very expensive* term life insurance, too costly a way to repay your car loan if you die. And dealers love to sell it because it is so profitable. But it is illegal for a dealer to insist you buy this insurance as a condition for a loan. If you do want to purchase insurance, buy it from an outside agency where you might save 50 percent...or more!

The leasing alternative

Leasing is an increasingly common alternative to conventional car financing. How does leasing differ from traditional financing? You finance a car to purchase it. Once the loan is repaid, you own the car.

When you lease a car you only pay to *use* the car. You never own it. During the lease you are responsible for its maintenance and upkeep. You drive it whenever and wherever you like, but cannot sell or dispose of it. At the end of the lease (usually 2 to 5 years) you return the car unless you exercise any option to purchase the car. This option, of course, must be included in the lease.

One great advantage from leasing is that your monthly payments are usually lower than if you financed-to-buy the car. Regardless of selling price, you pay only a portion of the car's price—that part that represents the depreciation on the car. For example, a $15,000 car worth $6,000 in five years, depreciates 60 percent over the lease. Your lease payments will be based upon this $9,000 in depreciated value over 5 years. This, with interest, is paid in monthly payments over the lease term. Monthly lease payments are generally lower than monthly finance charges because the financed amount is lower. Lease a car that depreciates slowly and your payments will be even lower.

Another variation to traditional leasing is to find someone who now leases a car but wants out of the lease. Negotiate to assume the lease. You'll find such ads in the classifieds, but realize that most car leases require that you obtain the permission of the leasing company to assume the lease. The leasing company, as legal owner, can otherwise declare the lease in default and repossess the car.

There are also companies that specialize in lease takeover deals. You lease from them and they pay the original lease. The original leaseholder usually remains liable to the leasing company. Examine these contracts carefully and make sure you fully understand them. These companies are listed in the classifieds automotive section.

Here are four more tips before you lease your car:

1) The value of the car at the end of the lease is partly based on the number of miles you drive. You are generally allowed 15,000 miles per year (or 45,000 in three years). You will be charged 10 to 20 cents per additional mile. A leased car returned with 100,000 miles on the odometer will cost you a hefty $5,500 penalty. Can you keep your mileage low?

2) Some dealerships depreciate the car from the full selling or sticker price. Depreciation, however, should be based upon the lowest price you could buy the car for if you paid cash. Compromise if you have poor credit, but know exactly how your monthly payments will be calculated, and what price and interest rate they are based upon. All are negotiable.

3) Your ability to qualify for a lease also partly depends upon the economy. Surprisingly, it is often easier to in tough economic times because dealerships are then under more pressure to move cars. In a weak economy it is usually easier to both lease and finance a car.

4) A lease also may require a substantial down payment or deposit. But as with financing, the larger the down payment, the lower the lease payments.

Turning poor credit into a home mortgage

Ready for a home? There are four basic lenders who will give you the money:

1) Traditional lenders: Include banks—who are most conservative, have the strictest lending requirements and qualifying formulas. Banks are reluctant to lend to poor credit risks. However, they often lessen their risk by selling their mortgage to other investors with more lenient requirements and more willing to assume greater risks. Once the mortgage is sold, the bank has recovered their loan and has no further risk. As a borrower, you now pay whomever owns your loan. Some banks do not sell their mortgages, so ask about your bank's policy.

2) Credit unions and hometown banks are more progressive than traditional banks and more than your past credit also consider your:

- current financial situation
- present ability to pay
- financial stability

While all lenders evaluate credit, you will probably have an opportunity to explain any remaining credit problems to these lenders. Highlight any accounts with a bank, or perhaps a secured loan to make your loan requirements more reasonable. You may be able to reach a compromise with a larger down payment or higher interest.

3) Mortgage brokers closely resemble both traditional and the more progressive lenders. Mortgage brokers are financial matchmakers between lending institutions and qualified borrowers.

Mortgage brokers represent the countless banks, lending institutions, organizations, and private individuals with money to loan. The National Association of Mortgage Brokers estimates their members handle about 50 percent of all mortgages. An experienced mortgage broker can accurately assess your chances of obtaining a mortgage, help with the paperwork and estimate its costs. But you will pay for this expertise and convenience as mortgage brokers charge a fee—often an advance payment of 2 to 5 percent—for finding you a loan. How do you find a good mortgage broker? Check the Yellow Pages and ask these four questions:

1. How many banks do you represent? Good brokers represent at least 10 banks nationwide, with most local lenders.

2. What is your firm's closing ratio? A closing ratio shows how successfully the broker places loans. 70 percent is a good ratio.

3. Can you supply local references? Check references very thoroughly.

4. Will you specify in writing the charges I will be responsible for? Compare brokers and carefully compare their respective charges.

4) Government agencies. The Federal Housing Authority (FHA) and the Veteran's Administration (VA) are the two chief lenders.

The FHA and the VA are actually insurers, not lenders. They guarantee your loan (or part of the loan) in case you default. If you qualify you can obtain an FHA loan with as little as a 5 percent down payment. You can obtain a VA mortgage with no down payment. To find out if you qualify for a FHA mortgage, contact a real estate broker, your local bank, credit union or the FHA.

The VA mortgage is only available to qualifying veterans. You may qualify as a veteran if you served on active duty for at least 90 days during World War II, or the Korean or Vietnam War, or served on active duty for at least 180 consecutive days before September 7, 1980, or served on active duty for at least 24 months after September 7, 1980.

Unlike an FHA mortgage, a VA mortgage only guarantees a loan up to $46,000. However, this is usually sufficient to protect the lender. VA guidelines are flexible. Contact your local VA office to obtain a certificate of eligibility.

The VA and the FHA both have assumable mortgages which enable you to take over a seller's mortgage. There are two types of assumable mortgages: Qualifying assumable mortgages are similar to traditional mortgages offered by traditional lenders. You must meet specific requirements to qualify for a loan. Non-qualifying assumable mortgages require only that you can meet the monthly payments.

Thirteen creative home-financing techniques

Are you still looking for that elusive mortgage? Then consider these thirteen even more powerful financing tools.

1) *Owner financing.* Sellers do finance their buyers. This provides monthly income for the seller and the seller can foreclose on the home if you default on your payments. Owners who are most anxious to sell will be most anxious to finance. But sometimes a seller has no mortgage and simply wants to use his mortgage as an investment. If the seller has an existing mortgage on the home, the seller's mortgage becomes a second mortgage.

   Credit requirements on a seller's mortgage are more lenient. Another advantage: You deal directly with the person making the decision, not some anonymous bank committee.

2) *State financing agencies.* You may be able to find low-interest home financing through your state's financing agency whose funding is raised through mortgage revenue bonds. These HUD supervised programs require that you must not have owned a home during the previous three years. Down payments are often 5 percent or less, and some state programs provide 100 percent financing. Contact the agency in your state for a free brochure on its loan programs.

3) *Equity sharing.* This arrangement demands a good attorney because it involves complex legal considerations. Here an investor buys and finances a home. You agree to occupy the home and pay the mortgage through a rental fee. You also maintain the home and agree to live in the home for a specified time at the end of which you can sell the house. Once the

house is sold, you reimburse the investor his initial contribution and divide the remaining profit between you. The investor knows that because you have an equity stake in the home, you will take care of it. You also receive part of the profits and deduct the interest portion of your mortgage payments, as well as your share of the property taxes from your income taxes.

4) *Co-signers.* Can you convince family or friends to guarantee your loan? Be careful. If you default, your co-signer becomes responsible for the loan. Many banks accept co-signers because they then have someone financially stable to sue in case of a default. A co-signed loan makes you responsible not only to yourself, but to your co-signer. But when there is no other place to turn, family or friends may be the answer.

5) *Borrow from your retirement or pension plan.* Your pension or profit-sharing plan can lend you money based upon your contribution to the plan. The law allows you to borrow up to one-half the vested amount (the money in the plan that you own) or $50,000, whichever is less. A plan can lend up to $10,000, regardless of vested amount. The loan term is limited to five years unless the loan is to purchase a principal residence. Then there is no term limit. Interest rates must be competitive. A pension plan is one of your most important assets. If you die or retire before the full amount of the loan is repaid, the outstanding balance will be deducted from your estate.

6) *Life insurance.* You can only borrow against the cash or surrender value of a whole life or permanent life insurance policy. Many policies let you borrow up to 95 percent of its value with no time limit to repay. The older the policy the lower the interest rate. Remember, your coverage under a policy is reduced by what you borrow. Outstanding balances and interest are also deducted from any distributions under the policy should you die. While this is an inexpensive way to borrow, consider this carefully. If you are receiving low

yields on the your life insurance, it may be smarter to cash in the policy and reinvest the money in your home.

7) ***Enlist your employer's financial help.*** Today many companies advance their employees a down payment to buy their homes. Repayment is deducted monthly from the employee's wages. Your employer may instead buy the home and lease it to you with an option to buy while the employer receives the tax benefits from ownership. Many companies have some variation of this plan in their employee incentive plans.

8) ***Form a syndicate.*** Why not organize a group for the purpose of investing in real estate? Investors are collectively secured by your mortgage and also get some equity or profits from the house.

9) ***Inheritance buy-outs.*** Do you have a trust or inheritance? If your inheritance is held in trust, or won't be available to you until later, you can sell your right to your inheritance or trust to companies who can wait for the funds to be released. A good mortgage broker can help you on this.

10) ***Pay the seller a 100 percent financing bonus.*** In exchange negotiate a lower interest rate and a longer term. This will keep your monthly payments to about what it would be with a normal down payment. You will pay the seller substantially more money over the term of the loan—but not substantially more per month!

11) ***Union financing.*** The AFL-CIO, for instance, offers first time home loans to affiliated union members who pay as little as 3 percent down. An additional 2 percent comes from the union-owned Amalgamated Bank of New York. Other union programs even eliminate the loan origination fees. Parents and children of union members also may qualify.

12) ***Probate properties.*** Yes, people do inherit homes that they do not want to live in. They then prefer to sell and pocket the money. Heirs are usually busy people and can be extremely motivated sellers, especially if

mortgage payments must be made on the home. The prospects of a regular monthly income may motivate them to sell with little or no cash down.

13) **Skill trading.** Why not trade you talents and skills for part of the down payment? Your talent may be valuable to the seller, and the seller may waive part of the price or down payment in exchange for what you can offer.

Seek a motivated seller. Sellers under pressure will help you to buy their home using little or none of your own money. But how do you find motivated sellers?

Courthouses and attorneys are good starting places. Check for divorces, partnership disagreements, building management problems, foreclosures, probate and estate sales, and financial problems.

Banks are especially good source for locating people with debt problems. Real estate agents also know who lost their jobs, are being transferred, or have financial problems, illnesses, or divorces. Accountants come across partnership problems, divorces, debt problems, lost jobs, and property management problems. And insurance companies know about probate and estate sales and job transfers. Of course, the sheriff's department is often the first to encounter serious problems. Finally, don't overlook the daily newspaper—a continuous source of information about people with every conceivable problem and need to sell...even to people with no credit.

Key points to remember

- You have better odds for financing a new car at a car dealership than at a bank or credit union.

- Choose a large, high volume car dealership, because they have the leverage to win approval of your application.

- Negotiate the car's price, interest rate and down payment even if you have shaky credit. Don't let bad credit make you the victim of a bad deal.

- Regardless of how you finance anything, the larger the down payment, the lower your monthly payments and this also applies to car financing.

- Examine such options to finance a car, as a co-signer, "straw man sale," or recourse loans.

- If you do finance a car from a Buy-Here, Pay-Here dealer, do consult the Blue Book first. Avoid a "rip-off" price because you're blinded by easy credit.

- Never buy credit life insurance from a car dealership.

- Consider the advantages of leasing a car. As a financing alternative, your monthly payments should be lower with leasing.

  But whether you lease or finance, always know how your monthly payments are calculated.

- Investigate companies that match unwanted auto leases to people who want to assume them.

- Whether for a car or a home, the more unconventional the lender, the easier it is to obtain credit.

- Mortgage brokers have access to lenders nationwide. They can often match you to your "right"loan.

- Investigate government lending agencies—such as the FHA and the VA. They provide several good financing programs, if you qualify.

Credit And
Financing
A Business

9

Credit And Financing A Business

It is considerably easier to finance the purchase of a going business than a startup because an existing business has both a track record and assets:

- Receivables
- Contracts
- Cash flow
- Fixtures and equipment
- Money in the bank

- Inventory
- Leases
- Trademark and patent rights
- Customer lists
- Real estate

Most business lenders are asset-based so these assets are valuable collateral. But a business that is nothing more than an idea is a very risky financing venture. You must be a super-salesman to convince someone to finance that idea. Unless you can demonstrate you have both the knowledge and experience necessary to turn the idea into a successful business it will be extremely difficult to find the money to launch that business. Buying an existing business, on the other hand, is always less difficult—even if you have little money or poor credit.

Where the money is

There are many financing sources for your business:

- Banks
- Sellers

- Time sharing
- Leases

- Suppliers
- Brokers
- SBA
- Inventory
- Sale-leaseback
- Accounts receivable
- Motor vehicles
- Life insurance
- Partners/investors
- Franchising

Each financing source is only one part of the overall financing puzzle and they are often used in combination to create 100 percent financing. Master these money sources. They can be your key to opportunity.

Bank financing

Banks are the most obvious source of external financing when you want to borrow money for a business. You probably already deal with a bank, even if its only a savings and checking account. But borrowing money to buy a business is much more complex than obtaining a home mortgage, a car loan or passbook savings loan. To obtain a business loan you must first forget four common myths:

Myth #1: *Banks are in business to lend money.* False! Banks are in business to make money. Money is their inventory and they use it to make profitable loans.

Myth #2: *Banks have standard loan policies.* This also is false. There is no "standard" loan policy. All loans are negotiable.

Myth #3: *Banks have unlimited loan funds.* Again false. Banks have limited money to lend and you must compete for those dollars. So banks chiefly lend money on the basis of security and safety in what is a highly competitive process.

Myth #4: *Banks do not need your business.* Fortunately, also false. Yes, you need a bank's money, but the bank equally needs your business.

For maximum success, start by choosing the right bank. Banks, like restaurants and retailers, do specialize. Business loans are best obtained from commercial banks, while home mortgages and consumer loans are the specialty of the savings banks and cooperatives. For a small loan (under $100,000), concentrate on small, local banks. They will view you differently than a large bank that routinely makes 10 million dollar loans. Local banks prefer to be close to their customers and more actively support small community-based businesses.

Approach the bank where your target business already has a relationship. Let the seller introduce you. Meet the president of the bank. Deal with someone with the authority to approve your loan and who can act decisively. Why waste time with a junior loan officer? The bank will make a handsome profit on your loan, so don't be intimidated.

To win financing you must act like a pro. Know what the bank will look for. Remember the three C's of loanmanship:

- *Character.* Does your credit history justify the loan?

- *Cash flow.* Does the business provide sufficient cash flow and profit to pay the loan?

- *Collateral.* How much risk will the bank have if you fail to repay the loan? Will the bank have the collateral needed to recover the loan?

How to draft a successful loan proposal

Follow the three C's of loanmanship and you can prepare a clear, logical and businesslike proposal.

I.   Credit and Personal History (Character)

Name and address

Family status

Employment history

Experiences in related business

Education

Personal assets

Personal liabilities

Military status

Bank references

Credit references

II. Financial Information on the Business (Cash Flow)

Brief description of the business

Brief history of the business

Tax returns for two years

Projected cash flow statement for loan period

Summary of proposed business changes

Lease or proposed lease terms

III. Collateral

Business assets

Acquisition cost or replacement cost

Liquidation value of assets

IV. Proposed Loan

Amount required

Loan period

Interest terms

Identification of guarantors

Collateral to be pledged

If you use this checklist to prepare your proposal, you will provide the banker with the answers necessary to evaluate your loan and also boost your credibility. Because you anticipated the banker's questions, you made his job easier and he then has more confidence in you because he knows you are a pro.

The information on your loan proposal must be complete and accurate. The numbers also must work. Have your accountant prepare the financial information (and join you in negotiations with the bank). Let the banker know that you are guided by another professional. Expect the banker to ask hard, probing questions to test your knowledge of the business. Be prepared!

Six tips to negotiate your perfect loan

Aggressively negotiate favorable loan terms. Follow these six rules and you will save big money on your loan.

1) *Negotiate interest.* Interest rates are *always* negotiable. If the bank agrees that your business plan is sound, it can drop the interest several points. This can save you many thousands of dollars.

2) *Demand the longest possible loan period.* This conserves cash by lowering your monthly payments.

3) *Pledge only business assets as collateral.* This protects your personal assets in the event of a loan default. Even if you have signed a personal guarantee and the business defaults, the proceeds from the auction may be sufficient to satisfy the bank.

4) *Never falsify the loan application.* Falsifying information can bring immediate foreclosure and prevent you from discharging your debt in bankruptcy and even bring criminal charges.

5) *Never borrow personally.* Your corporation must borrow the money, not you. If you personally borrow the money, then the bank cannot claim the business assets if you default. You will then have to repay the loan personally. Obtain the help of an attorney on this.

6) *Never settle for the first loan offer.* There are plenty of banks. Shop for the best deal and compare.

How to borrow your down payment

Borrowing your down payment requires a different strategy than arranging a long term loan with a hefty down payment. Bankers want you to use your own money to match theirs when you buy the business. Conversely, your down payment loan will be short term (usually for one year or less) and typically for about 20 percent of the purchase price. You cannot pledge the business assets to the bank as collateral because they will probably be pledged to a lender who financed the lion's share of the price. The secret then is never to reveal to the bank that you need the loan for a down payment on the business. Instead, try these perfectly legal techniques to raise your down payment.

- *Borrow multiple loans simultaneously.* This strategy legally increases your borrowing power five- to ten-fold. Even with limited personal assets, if you can obtain a small unsecured loan, perhaps $2,000, only on your signature, then five banks should collectively loan you $10,000. Of course, once you receive the first loan, you must disclose it on later credit applications. But if you simultaneously apply for loans at five banks, you can truthfully state that you have no other outstanding loans. This effectively increases your borrowing power. This technique won't work if the application asks about "loans applied for." Fortunately, few ask this question.

- *Tap the power of pyramid loans.* The pyramid strategy involves two banks and some beginning capital—say $3,000. Here too, you will borrow $3,000 on your signature alone following these easy steps: First, apply for a $3,000 loan payable in 30 days at a local bank. Then place these loan proceeds in a high-interest bearing account at another bank. In 25 days withdraw the $3,000 and pay your first bank. About two weeks later return to the first bank and apply for a $6,000 loan. You'll probably receive it because you now have good credit. Invest the $6,000 and again repay the loan in 25 days. Finally, in the third month repeat the entire process with a $10,000 loan. Pay it ahead of schedule and the bank will gladly lend you $15,000. Each loan fortifies your credit rating and your borrowing power. Soon you have your down payment.

- *Find a co-signer,* perhaps a friend or relative. This request is often easier for them to grant than asking them to actually make the loan.

Once you have your down payment, loan it to your business. You then quickly repay yourself and pay the bank. You will have eliminated your investment risk, released whatever collateral you pledged, and improved your credit rating. Most importantly, you will have a no cash down deal.

Rig the deal for total financing

You can even borrow 100 percent of the purchase price of a business from a bank. How is this possible when banks usually lend only 50-60 percent of the purchase price? Consider that a small business is difficult to accurately appraise. You can therefore often increase the purchase price of the business in order to obtain a higher loan. How can this be legal? You might increase the purchase price on the contract and decrease the consideration on the non-compete agreement. Suppose the seller wants $50,000 for the business and $50,000 for an agreement not to compete with you. The bank may only be willing to lend you $25,000 or 50 percent of the selling price of the business itself. If you increase the selling price to $100,000 and reduce the non-compete agreement to $1.00, you will wind up with $50,000 for the business on a 50 percent loan. $50,000 is exactly the amount of money you need. This does not suggest that you should ever deliberately mislead a lender, and you certainly should have an attorney guide you to avoid legal problems.

Why seller financing may be your best bet

Seller financing is often the very best money source for buying a business. Many financial experts will advise you to ignore other sources until the seller has given his final "no." This is because seller financing features five big advantages:

1) *Sellers are less "interest-hungry."* Sellers do not finance to earn interest. They finance to sell their business. A smart seller realizes that this may be the only way to make a deal. A highly motivated seller may even finance you with dramatically cut interest payments. You are still likely to pay a higher rate than the seller could receive on his money from a bank, so the seller will still earn a profit on his loan. However, the seller chiefly wants to sell his business. Remember, every point you save on interest puts money in your pocket!

2) *Sellers will wait longer for their money.* Banks typically want their money in five years. But the longer the loan period the

smaller the payments. This obviously puts less strain on your cash flow and lets your business grow faster. Not even friends or relatives are likely to agree to long payouts, but sellers often extend notes for seven to ten years. Even 15 to 20 year rates are common. For these sellers financing creates an annuity.

3) *Sellers will finance more of the price.* Sellers know what their business is worth because they have their money tied up in it. They don't have to be as cautious as banks because if you do default the seller can easily step in and take back the business. The seller can more easily resell the business, while a bank or other lender must liquidate the business. So sellers can afford to be more lenient on how much of the price they will finance. Your goal? 70-100 percent seller financing.

4) *Sellers will not demand outside personal collateral.* Why? The seller has the best collateral in the world—his own business. Sellers seldom have the nerve to demand additional collateral. You may have to offer personal guarantees, and the seller will want a mortgage on the business, but you have a powerful argument for refusing personal collateral. "If the business isn't adequate collateral for your $50,000 loan, it's not worth the $65,000 I'm paying you for it!" It's a persuasive argument.

5) *Sellers can be more forgiving.* Sellers understand the nature of their own business. If business is slow and you miss a payment or two, a seller is apt to be more forgiving than will banks where the entire chain of command panics over a "problem loan." A seller has no one breathing down his neck and he is not as likely to impatiently foreclose. Perhaps, the seller was once in the same embarrassing position. Sellers understand cash flow problems and you can usually reason with them. And now that the business is finally sold, do you think the seller really wants it back?

While seller financing is a wonderful way to finance the purchase of a business, sooner or later you run headlong into seller's block, as when you are at the negotiating table and the seller suddenly freezes upon realizing that you are taking over his beloved business with everybody's money but your own. He then begins to resist the deal. Do let this neither surprise nor discourage you. A seller may be ashamed to admit to his spouse or friends that he gave up his business to someone who invested so little of his own money. Some sellers recall *their* hard-earned cash invested in the business, and now resent you as that smarter buyer. If you do encounter seller's block, try to find out what the problem is and stress some facts:

1) Ask the seller what he or she wanted from the deal. Isn't he getting it? If the seller is getting exactly what he wanted, why should it matter whether the money is coming from you?

2) If the seller is financing the deal, show the seller how he is protected. Convince the seller the security is adequate if you do default. A seller must see little risk.

3) Highlight your investment. No, it may not be your own money on the line, but what about your personal guarantees, or what you stand to lose on a default? This demonstrates your financial commitment and cancels seller suspicions.

4) Finally, share with the seller your plans for the business. Have the seller see the time and effort you will spend to improve the business.

Let suppliers finance your business

Your suppliers may make as much, or even more money from your business as you. Since they too will benefit from your business why not have them contribute to your venture? Once they see their profit potential from your business, they may eagerly advance you your down payment. Supplier financing works well with any business that purchases inventory. Key suppliers are the logical financing sources because they will reap the biggest rewards from your business. Suppliers have small risk from financing if they are adequately secured with business assets. Don't be shy. If you succeed you will sell *their* products and *earn* them many times their investment for many years to come.

How do you get a supplier loan? First, convince the supplier that it will be mutually beneficial. Zero-in on the business' primary suppliers. Most businesses purchase most of their inventory from only a few suppliers. Secondary or "fill in" suppliers are poor loan candidates. Target primary suppliers that are themselves family-owned businesses. They have more flexibility to make customer loans than do large, national firms.

Estimate the annual business you can give the supplier. What is the supplier's gross profit on that merchandise? Now negotiate. Your deal is for your supplier to lend you money in exchange for your profitable business. Don't be afraid to ask for a loan that equals about six month's worth of projected profits to the supplier. The more competitive your industry, the more you can request. Of course, your supplier will want to be paid quickly, and never accept a loan unless it can be safely repaid from future cash flow. Your supplier also will be greatly concerned about the safety of his loan, so offer a mortgage on the businesses assets and, if necessary, your personal guarantee. Your supplier also will expect your agreement to purchase a minimum amount of merchandise over a specified time. Failure to comply may cause a loan default.

Let your supplier see you in the best possible light. Let him visualize how he will benefit from your growing business. Let him know you will feature his most profitable lines. Detail your expansion plans. Highlight his prior profitable relationship with the business. Recruit a few of the supplier's major customers to endorse you. The supplier may accommodate you to please them. Remember, buying power is borrowing power! Existing suppliers lend for fear of *losing* a good account. Prospective suppliers lend to *win* new business. In either case, the supplier who foresees that the loan will yield exceptional dividends is a supplier ready to open his checkbook.

How to turn the broker's commission into your down-payment

Business brokers handle about two out of three businesses sold. So you have a solid opportunity to have your broker help you with your financing. How? Recruit your broker as your partner in the down payment. Consider that a 20 percent down payment is about average on any deal. Brokers receive 10 percent of the selling price as their commission. The commission then amounts to about half the down payment. So convince the broker that you can finance most of the purchase price but cannot raise the entire down payment. The broker may then agree to loan you part of his commission rather than lose the sale and all of his commission. But play fair with the broker. Quickly repay the loan. Pay interest and secure the loan with collateral.

Use the brokers commission gambit when there is *no* broker! How? Simply ask the seller to reduce the price (and the down payment) by showing the seller how much less he may have pocketed *had* a broker been involved. This is a powerful negotiating tactic.

Customers will bankroll you

Customer financing works beautifully with certain businesses. Does your target business offer a unique product or service? Does it serve a particular market or group of customers? If so, your customers may pay you in advance for what you can offer them. For example, advance subscriptions to a new magazine may give a publisher the capital to print and mail the first several issues. Or a medical company with a new animal vaccine may borrow its start up costs against advance orders from thousands of veterinarians. A Chinese restaurant may rent its largest dining room to bridge clubs during the day. There are thousands of similar stories. One particularly popular version is the concept of the "super co-op"—where many small retailers within an industry ban together to buy cooperatively. Their huge volume ensures them lower prices, better terms, and the profits needed to compete against national chains. The retailers contribute capital to join the co-op, which then purchases merchandise for its members. Customers can be the best money source to finance your business.

The truth about borrowing from Big Brother

The Small business Administration (SBA) says its mission "is to help people get into business and stay in business." They guarantee loans made by banks to small businesses; "independently owned and operated, and not dominant in their field." This doesn't mean you must stay small, but only be small when you apply for the loan.

The SBA rarely makes direct loans, unless your business is in a badly depressed area. More typically, money is loaned by a local bank and the SBA guarantees 90 percent of the loan. Because the loan is largely guaranteed, these banks can resell the loan at a lower interest rate and pocket the difference.

Most SBA loans are *not* approved. To qualify, you must prove that you were rejected by two private lenders. So the weak loan gets approved. The most frequent reason the SBA rejects a loan application is lack of business experience and a poor business plan. According to the SBA, a good business plan specifies:

- The purpose of the loan
- The amount of the loan
- How your cash flow will repay the loan
- A description of the business
- Profit and loss statements for the last three years
- An operating forecast for the loan term
- Your personal balance sheet, and your personal investment in the business
- Partners or stockholders owning more than 20 percent of the company, and their personal financial statements and credit histories
- Business and personal assets offered as collateral
- Market research that shows why your business will succeed
- Your lease agreement
- Resumes for each top manager

SBA loans generally run from 7 to 20 years, and this is a great advantage over a bank's shorter loans because a longer payback greatly helps ease cash flow.

The SBA also does not demand strong credit because it is committed to start where the banks stop. Moreover the SBA strongly favors minority groups and primarily lends to businesses in distressed areas. Banks will generally not.

The SBA also provides management, financial and production counselling and gives special consideration to veterans, their survivors and dependents.

Not all is rosy with SBA loans.

- The SBA demands extensive personal collateral. They will mortgage your home.
- The SBA can take up to six months to process a loan.
- The SBA will expect you to match revenues so you may need to put up about one half of the purchase price yourself. Like banks, the SBA discourages secondary financing or high-leverage deals but even more so!

But don't stop if you strike out with the SBA. Uncle Sam probably has the right loan for you. The federal government has more than 1,000 loan programs to finance small businesses. Inquire at your local SBA office. If they can't help you, they may direct you to more suitable governmental programs.

The ABC's of inventory financing

Another way to finance your down payment is to look for excess inventory that can be quickly sold without hurting the business. Suggest that instead of your down payment, the seller sell the excess inventory and apply the proceeds to his down payment. A common variation is the "simultaneous sell-off" where a buyer in a similar business buys the excess inventory once you buy the business.

Many businesses have more inventory than they need to maintain sales. *Your* down payment may be sitting on the shelf!

Financing from cash flow

One great way to raise your down payment is to squeeze the businesses' cash flow. The average business does enough business in two or three weeks to cover its down payment. Your strategy then is to have this cash flow finance the down payment *after* you buy the business.

First, calculate surplus cash flow by subtracting projected expenses from cash receipts over the first several weeks. This is cash available to pay to the seller for the down payment. Project conservatively. Underestimate, don't overestimate the available money.

To maximize cash flow, defer every possible expense. Forecast how long you can delay suppliers. Return excess or unsaleable merchandise to vendors for credit. Negotiate more lenient credit terms with suppliers. Every dollar in credit is a dollar you can offer the seller for the down payment.

Or convince the seller to withhold payments to his suppliers. The business' debts may rise, but the seller can take this cash for the down payment. You will assume and eventually pay these supplier debts but for now you have a business with no cash down!

Remember, while every seller wants an all-cash deal, sellers don't care where the money comes from. Borrow from a bank, relatives, creditors, or even the seller's own business. Just get him the cash!

To make the seller more comfortable with cash flow financing, hand him postdated checks for the down payment. This gives the seller no more legal protection than a short-term promissory note, but a check is psychologically comforting. People are wary of promissory notes and will more likely respect your personal check as payment in hand.

The sale-leaseback strategy

Equipment and real estate also can generate your down payment via a sale-leaseback. Example: A small family owned pool cleaning service sold for $100,000. Its assets included four trucks and equipment worth $50,000, and the good will from 100 accounts generating seasonal revenues of $150,000. The seller asked $100,000 for the business with $35,000 down. At the closing the buyer sold the trucks to investors for $35,000 who then leased the trucks to the buyer for $700 per month. The buyer had his $35,000 down payment from the seller's trucks!

The sale-leaseback works with any type equipment or even real estate, but computers, high-technology items, material handling-equipment and motor vehicles are prime assets for a sale-leaseback.

Or why not time share your business? Time sharing under-used equipment is another way to a down payment. Suppose the business has a computer or printing press that is seldom used. Why not rent it to others when its not working for you? If your equipment can handle two or three times the work you demand from it, you may be able to collect substantial rents by leasing it to others. Time sharing gets you your down-payment if your time sharing customers will prepay their rental fee. Offer them a substantial prepayment discount. The customer saves money and you have your down payment.

The business asset to target may be neither its inventory nor equipment, but its lease. The right location can turn any businesses into a money-machine for a down payment. How? Enter into an advance agreement to sublease part of your space and collect advance rent (offer a discount if necessary). It has worked for countless entrepreneurs! Only your imagination limits the possibilities.

Idle space can produce big results. Do you have billboard space? Negotiate a lease with a major billboard company. They pay big advances. An idle parking lot? Turn it into immediate cash. For example, an evening restaurant might profitably lease the lot during the day.

Turn accounts receivable into fast-cash

Accounts receivable is cash that flows into your business. So if your target business has $20,000 in receivables, and the seller wants $20,000 for a down payment you can see two immediate solutions: Give the seller the accounts receivable in place of the down payment (the receivables will generate cash for the seller in

30 to 60 days and you will not have to collect yourself) or "factor" the accounts receivable. A factor buys your receivables for about 90 percent of their face value. Turning this "immediate" cash over to the seller decreases the down payment *you* need.

Partners for profit

Regardless of their number, or what they invest, all partners share one point: Once aboard, you work for them! You no longer work only for yourself. If you are that individual who wants to share responsibility and decisions—and can't raise money any other way—then consider a partner. But if you need *only* a partner's money, then move cautiously. Partnership money is mighty expensive money. Your partner's small investment may cost you many times that amount over the years. Beg or borrow money from wherever you can, but make a partner *your last* resort for raising capital.

If you do sincerely want a partner, then distinguish the good from the bad. Examine your potential partner's work history. Is it a solid work record? Is he a "doer" or a "drifter"? Does he have needed management skills? Does he command your confidence? Look for stability! And what about your future partner's personal history? Poor health can pose major problems, as can personal weaknesses, such as gambling or drinking.

Investigate all the skeletons in his closet. Has he been in other business deals? How did they work out? What do his prior partners say about him? And what about personal lifestyles? A clash of lifestyles can cause huge partnership problems. And evaluate your partner's spouse. Spouses influence their mates. A perfect partner may have an interfering spouse. That can destroy the partnership.

Can your partner match your financial resources? He may match your down payment but can he raise the money to help the business grow? Why mortgage *your* house because your partner has nothing to offer? Be as careful with a partner considerably wealthier than yourself. You may find yourself on the short end of a squeeze play. You may be the brains behind the business, but money always wins! Finally, are your ideas compatible concerning growth, responsibility, and finances?

Your partner may be a close college friend or business acquaintance. You may have answered a newspaper ad from someone with capital to invest. Or perhaps placed your own ad for a partner. Whenever you approach someone for money, you must sell him on your business idea. Whether starting from scratch or buying an existing business, you need a business proposal that contains:

1) *Company background*: Its history, organization, current financial statements, and legal structure (sole proprietorship, corporation, etc.)

2) *Management:* Their backgrounds and accomplishments. Show that the company has effective management. For investors, good management is as important as a good business concept.

3) *Competitive advantages:* Outline why the company, product, or service is unique.

4) *Competition:* Analyze your competitors. How do their products compare with yours?

5) *Marketing:* Identify your market segment. Who are your customers? Describe advertising, promotion and sales costs. Detail how your product is distributed to your markets.

6) *Finances:* Project your financial statements over several years. Work with an accountant on this.

7) *Investment:* How will you use the money you seek? Will additional funds be needed and where will it come from? How will you raise money for expansion?

8) *The deal:* Sell the investment in terms of safety, return on investment, and growth potential.

Review your proposal. Can you back it up with hard facts? To discover how much you really know about your business, investors will try to pick your plan apart. They won't open their wallets unless you can convince them that you know your business.

Also create a formula to buy out your partner if you should disagree. Also demand at least 51 percent ownership for voting control. If your partner insists on a 50-50 deal, try to obtain voting control by having your partner assign to you the right to vote some of his shares.

Join the franchise boom

Financing is one big benefit of joining a franchise system. Franchisers routinely finance 60-70 percent of the start-up cost. They may also guarantee your bank loan or make a direct loan. But the better franchise systems demand excellent credit from their franchisees.

Because a franchiser can easily reclaim a mismanaged franchised business, a franchiser can offer more generous finance terms. If the franchiser offers a $120,000 package with $20,000 down and financing for $100,000, you can be certain the franchiser can resell the business for $100,000 if you don't make the grade.

Key points to remember:

- Know what the bank will look for in a business loan: credit, cash flow and collateral.
- Negotiate and structure the business loan to your benefit.
- Seller financing has advantages over bank financing. Start with the seller.
- You can get the seller to finance with no-cash down even if you have poor or no personal credit.
- Sell suppliers on financing you in terms of the "suppliers profit," and what your account should mean to him. But negotiate a supplier loan that is fair for both sides.
- Brokers end up with a big slice of every down payment. Ask the broker to loan you half the commission so he can pocket the other half.

- Prepaid customer deposits can give you all the advance money you need to buy or start a solid business.

- Watch the pitfalls—as well as benefits—before signing a government loan.

- Hidden assets such as leases, excess inventory, equipment, accounts receivable, and motor vehicles can provide you with the down payment for your business.

- Select a partner for more than financial reasons. Retain at least 51 percent of the voting shares in the business so you stay in control.

- Franchisers are a potential source of funding, if franchised business can satisfy your business goals, and if you have good credit.

25 Credit Scams To Avoid

25 Credit Scams To Avoid

People who are most anxious for credit are those most vulnerable to credit scams. Most credit scams are clearly illegal. Others stack the deck so heavily against the borrower that while legal, they are simply unconscionable.

Credit scams prey upon ignorance and desperation. Some of the largest corporations in America are nothing more than sophisticated pool hall loan sharks who routinely fleece their clients. Because credit is big business, all the pressure that Madison Avenue and modern technology can bring to bear is used to convince you to sign on the dotted line and enter into a credit "deal" that is rarely in your best interests.

Your only defenses? Patience. Knowledge. Suspicion. Learn to be patient-even when desperate. And understand thoroughly anything that requires your signature. Aggressively question. Be an educated skeptic!

Exposing the 25 worst credit scams

There are as many credit scams as ways to lend money or extend credit. While some are elaborate "stings" practiced by professional cons, most credit scams are of the garden-variety and more easily detected.

Credit rackets flourish because they cater to the two basic elements to every credit scam—fear and greed. We are each motivated by the fear that we will be denied something we need, want, or deserve. We also are motivated by greed, or the desire to get something we want for nothing. These two powerful motivators often blind even the most honest and sensible. Thousands of credit-scam complaints to Better Business Bureaus each month prove the point. What about *you*? Have you been taken by one of these scams?

1) *Catalogue credit cards.* Issued by mail order catalog companies, these cards allow you to purchase from their company's catalog. Often called "gold" or "platinum" cards, they sound like bank credit cards, but are not. You will be offered a high credit line without any credit check. And if this offer sounds too good to be true, it is.

Why?

- The merchandise in their fancy catalogues is overpriced by 50 percent or more, so you vastly overpay for the credit.

- You must make a large down payment (between 40-85 percent of the price) to cover the seller's product cost. The company thus loses nothing by offering extensive credit—even with no credit checks—because later payments become pure profit to the seller.

- Other credit offers inevitably accompany the cards: expensive application, memberships, or order processing fees. And while these companies claim there are no interest charges, the interest is hidden within the inflated price.

These catalog companies seldom report to credit bureaus, so despite their claims, you cannot rebuild credit by dealing with them. They are simply a *very easy* way to obtain *expensive* products with very expensive credit!

2) *Telephone credit scams.* Here 900 or 976 numbers are leased from the phone companies by other companies that want to sell you a product or service by phone. But call these numbers and you pay an additional charge above the normal call costs. This charge can top 20 dollars per minute!

How does this relate to *your* credit? Because credit is the item most commonly advertised by companies who use these 900 or 976 phone numbers, they may invite you to call their 900 or 976 number to obtain a secured bankcard or catalogue credit card. But all you then receive for your money is a credit application— plus a very large phone bill.

3) *Advance-fee loans.* While illegal in many states, hundreds of thousands of people are still victimized by this scam each year. In its simplest form, someone promises to find you a loan in exchange for an advance fee. This person may call himself a loan broker. However, after you pay this advance fee, the broker disappears with your money.

Legitimate loan brokers usually collect their fee *after* they obtain your loan, with their fee paid from the loan. An advance-fee loan broker, in contrast, collects *before* the loan is found.

There are many sophisticated techniques used to get you sucked into this scam. You might answer an ad from a professional sounding firm urging you to call a 976 number for more information, or to receive an application. The price of the call could be the fee or you may be asked to pay the fee by credit card, check or money order. These advance-brokers frequently advertise via cable television, radio, newspaper, flyers and handouts.

Before you hand your money over to such a broker, contact the Better Business Bureau, your state Consumer Protection Agency and the Federal Trade Commission. Remember, it is virtually impossible to recover your money if the broker fails to deliver. Be suspicious of anyone who asks you to pay for services before delivery.

4) *Bogus credit repair companies.* These companies promise to fix your credit often for an exorbitant fee that can run into thousands of dollars.

Remember, a credit repair company cannot do anything more than you can do yourself through patience, persistence and knowledge. And you can do it for far less than it will cost with a credit repair company. With this book at your fingertips you need not risk the expense of an outside credit repair company, whether reputable or shady.

Credit repair companies often disguise themselves as a legitimate financial-aid company, debt counselling service, loan consolidation company, or credit-fix-it company. Look for certain warning signs when you investigate one of these companies. These include such impossible claims and false promises in the company's advertising, as "No credit beyond repair," "Eliminate all negative reporting including bankruptcies," or "We can get you unlimited credit now, no matter how poor your credit history." Or the company claims it can get you a major bankcard even if you have poor or no credit. Or the company refuses to provide you with a detailed, written description of its services and policies before you sign a contract.

Credit repair companies use many techniques to draw clients: from court reported bankruptcies and telemarketing to direct mail advertising. Once they contact you, they often prey upon your fears with lies and deceptions:

- For starters, they may claim the company is affiliated with the federal government. In truth, beyond passing laws to protect consumers from unfair credit practices, the federal government is in no way connected with any aspect of credit repair.

- They may tell you that file segregation is a legal credit repair technique. But file segregation is an *illegal* technique used by some companies to create a separate identity for a client. This is a federal crime that may also involve mail or wire fraud. You may also be sued for civil fraud.

- They may also trade on your fear that bankruptcy destroys your ability to obtain credit for ten years. This also is not true. Most creditors consider bankruptcy case by case, and take into account the reason for the bankruptcy, and whether it was due to circumstances beyond your control, such as illness or job loss.

These misrepresentations are designed to panic you into seeking their help. The more desperate you view your situation, the more you will believe their extravagant claims.

Fifteen states have laws that regulate credit repair companies: Arkansas, California, Connecticut, Florida, Georgia, Louisiana, Maryland, Massachusetts, Nevada, New York, Oklahoma, Texas, Utah, Virginia and Washington. These states usually require credit repair companies to be bonded (or have insurance to cover up-front deposits in case they are sued by clients), abide by the FCRA, inform clients of their legal rights, provide clients with a written contract and allow clients 3 to 5 days to change their mind after they sign a contract.

Disguised as a debt consolidation company, the credit repair company also may offer you a very high interest loan with large up-front fees, possibly secured with your home as collateral.

Also disguised as a debt counseling service may be a bankruptcy attorney using the service as a "front" to attract clients. Another firm may offer you a national bankcard which is only a secured bankcard easily obtained yourself without having to pay an additional fee to the credit repair firm.

What should you do if you do decide to work with a credit repair firm? First, contact the Federal Trade Commission, Better Business Bureau, state's attorney general or the Department of Consumer Affairs to see if complaints have been filed, or legal action taken against the company. Second, meet personally with a representative of the company. Have the company tell you what it can and cannot do for you and get it in writing. Finally, do not under any circumstances give the company money in advance.

5) *Credit card cash advances and cash advance checks.* These scams are used by some banks to force you into a high interest loan. Here's how it works: You try to cash a check at a branch of the bank where you have your account. The teller refuses because it is against bank policy to cash checks from its other branches, so he suggests that the bank instead give you a cash advance on your bankcard. But of course, you may pay a huge advance fee to the bank for issuing the card, and also pay high interest from the minute you receive the money because

banks often eliminate the interest-free period with cash advances. If the bank eliminates the interest free period because of the cash advance, it can do so for the entire balance of your bill. You could therefore pay as much as 285 percent interest, even though you fully paid the entire cash advance within 30 days. Some banks will charge you additional interest on any unpaid balance in your credit card account. This ploy is known as pyramiding.

Cash advance checks work exactly the same as credit card advances. Madison Avenue has given them fancy names, but they are still only another way of using your credit card. The charges still appear on your monthly credit card bills and are subject to the same unconscionable interest rates.

6) *Overdraft protection.* This so-called "protection" can easily destroy you financially and is a variation of the cash advance scam. Here's how it works: If you write a check that exceeds your account balance, the bank honors the check and charges the difference to your credit card account. The bank will point out that since you avoided bouncing a check you avoided a bounced check fee.

But here's what you will pay: Because "protection" is usually rounded to the nearest 100 dollars, if you exceed the balance in your checking account by even 5 cents, the bank advances you the full 100 dollars. You are now also liable for all the other costs associated with credit card cash advances. The bank will apply the extra $99.95 it forced you to borrow and reduce your credit card account, while the bank collects interest on your "loan."

7) *"We waived your minimum monthly payment"* is one of the credit card companies most pernicious scams and is ever popular at times of increased spending, such as Christmas. Even though no minimum payment is required that month, you will continue to accrue interest. If you do take advantage of this offer, you simply increase your debt. If your debt is already high, and you accept this offer several times a year (sometimes you will receive this offer for six consecutive months), you will seriously increase your debt and make the bankcard company considerably wealthier. A minimum payment plan (an average of 18 percent

interest with a 2.5 percent minimum payment) will have you pay $4,230.83 on a $2,000 debt over the 12 years and 9 months it will take you to pay it down. Imagine how much longer it will take, and how much more it will cost if every one of those 12 years includes months in which you omit the minimum payment.

A popular variation is when you walk into a store in August to buy a big ticket item and the salesperson explains that if you buy the item today, you need not make payments until January. What the salesperson doesn't mention is that January's bill will include finance charges from August.

8) *Insurance from your credit card issuer.* Insurance offered by a credit card issuer is usually unnecessary and always overpriced! The terms are the worst to be found anywhere, whether it be life insurance, disability, unemployment, hospital insurance or any other type of coverage. If you want insurance, see an insurance broker who is independent of any bankcard. Be particularly skeptical about credit insurance. Banks love to sell this overpriced insurance because the banks are the beneficiaries as the payment is used to pay your outstanding balance if you die, while they collect hefty premiums in the interim.

9) *Credit card registration services.* These companies offer you protection from loss of your credit cards with just one phone call. But ask yourself, how often in your lifetime are you likely to lose all of your credit cards? If you pay 15 dollars a year for this protection, it will ultimately cost you hundreds of dollars to avoid a few toll-free phone calls. And each time you add or subtract a credit card from your list you must still notify the registration service by mail and store that correspondence. It is far easier and cheaper to keep your own records and notify the credit card companies yourself.

10) *Mail order loans.* Some bank will eventually send you a non-negotiable check. Simply fill out the short application and the bank will send you a real check for the stated amount. Beware. This is only another cash-advance mail order scheme. The bank will tempt you with very low minimum monthly payments, but the annual interest is likely to be the highest possible legal rate.

For instance, a $3,000 loan at 1.8 percent interest per month and paid in monthly installments of 2 percent will take 77 years and 3 months to fully pay. And you will have paid $24,734.58 in finance charges. Why else would the bank offer to lend you more money?

11) *Advance tax-refunds.* This loan is against an anticipated tax refund and only begins to make sense if you have a large tax refund. Why? This is because the fee you are charged is computed on an annualized rate, as though you borrowed the money for an entire year. But you may be borrowing the money for only four weeks. If you expect a $1,100 refund and pay a flat fee of $84 you are paying an effective annual interest rate of 92 percent. However, if you expect a $3,000 refund, the annualized rate drops to only 12 percent.

12) *Second mortgage scams* are most-common to the home improvement industry where con men offer to make home improvements in poor neighborhoods to people with considerable equity in their homes. They are always prime targets of this scam. The contractor arranges financing for his victims with lenders who offer second mortgages with very high interest rates and loan origination fees. Sometimes a contractor can convince the home owner to sign a trust deed to secure the work on the home. Even if the owner is dissatisfied with the work, the contractor can force the sale of the home to collect his money. Also avoid contractors who offer "package deals" which usually involve kickbacks.

13) *Bait and switch conversion loans.* Here unscrupulous loan brokers offer you a below market rate mortgage—if you first accept a mortgage loan with very high interest. You are promised that it will be converted to a lower interest mortgage, but until that happens you must continue to pay the interest. Beware. Conversion to the low-interest loan seldom happens.

14) *Waiving your rights.* Always read finance agreements carefully. Some agreements contain clauses stating that in the event of legal action, the consumer waives all legal defenses. Never waive your *legal* rights. You absolutely need them in the credit game!

15) *Illegal finance charges.* Any credit card issuer that provides an interest free grace period must mail your bill at least 14 days before interest is due. This gives you the chance to pay the bill without incurring a finance charge. If you receive the bill too late you are essentially forced to accept a finance charge—and this is illegal.

16) *Invasion of privacy.* While not a scam, it is a serious credit problem and one that continues to grow. This usually involves a technique called prescreening—or prequalification for credit.

Here's how this happens. Suppose the issuer of a new bankcard wants to find people with perfect credit who also earn at least $50,000 per year. The credit bureau, from their own files, can generate a list of potential customers featuring those qualifications. The company can also send its own list to the credit bureau, and the credit bureau can delete non-qualifying names. You may be on this list with neither your knowledge nor consent. Companies can then uncover your financial characteristics without seeing your actual credit report. The only way you can discover this is by inspecting your own credit report. If the word "promotional" or letters "prm" appear in the "inquiries" section, it means your file was prescreened. However, when a company sends you an unsolicited offer of credit or insurance, they must also give you a toll-free number to call; calling this number removes you from that creditor's list for up to two years. You can also directly request a credit bureau to omit you from their pre-screening lists, and in this case, you'll be off their lists indefinitely.

Other examples of irresponsible data collection:

- A company maintains a computerized list of persons who file malpractice suits against doctors and hospitals. This list enables medical personnel to screen out potential "troublemakers."

- A company keeps an index of patients who don't pay their bills, and hotel guests who damage or steal property and don't pay their lodging bills.

- A company that offers landlords "inside information" on tenants.

These bureaus and services do not notify you when your name is used by a third party. You are thereby denied your right to question the agency and have them reinvestigate. This is illegal because it violates the FCRA.

17) *Suicide rollovers.* This scam plays on the pressure of mounting debt and pretends to be a simple debt reliever: Take a cash advance from one credit card and use it to repay other credit cards. The more credit cards you have, the more credit cards you can manipulate. No cash is required. And if you have a large portfolio of credit cards you can continue to make minimum payments for a long while.

In the credit business these are called "suicide rollovers" because instead of facing your debt, you choose to commit financial suicide. This scheme contains most of the negative points discussed in the other scams. You don't buy time, you simply buy more debt and gain more creditors. Some financial advisors even suggest that in "good times" you obtain as many credit cards as possible so you will be prepared for the "tough times." This is one dangerous trap on the road to sound credit management.

18) *Shotgunning credit applications.* This is just dumb. You only end up with a massive inquiry list on your credit report and that will further hurt your chances for credit. Still, this is recommended by some credit advisors who should know better.

19) *Debt consolidation.* You apply for more credit to combine your debts into one payment. However, this immediately signals to a lender that you cannot meet your monthly payments. Additionally, interest rates are usually high or you must put up collateral to guard against default. This is a *good* strategy if you can repay the loan, but a *bad* strategy if you cannot.

20) *Mortgage reduction information kits.* These expensive kits which cost hundreds of dollars, and are peddled door to door, contain no information that you cannot find elsewhere for free or a few dollars. They all tell you the same

thing: cut your mortgage payments into bi-weekly installments to save interest! The problem is that only a few banks will accept bi-weekly payments.

21) ***Pre-payment penalties.*** This costly provision, usually found in the fine print of a loan agreement, is designed to keep you forever in debt. If you should fully pay the loan before it is due, the lender then forces you to pay a penalty. To pay a 5 percent penalty of the remaining $50,000 on your mortgage will cost you an extra $2,500. Negotiate this *out* of the contract! Also find out if your state restricts this type of clause. Many do.

22) ***Prepaid interest.*** The fine print may also include an "add-on-interest" clause. Such interest is added to the *total* amount of your loan *before* the lender calculates your monthly payments. The total amount of the loan is then divided by the number of required payments. There is no advantage to discharging the loan early, because the fine print says interest will not be refunded, so you would not save if you pay early. For example, if you borrow $5,000 and the interest for the term of the loan is $500, your total loan is $5,500, whether you pay in 20 months or two months.

23) ***Uncapped variable interest rates*** are also dangerous to your financial health. A capped variable interest rate is an interest rate that fluctuates with the prime interest rate, but never rises above a certain point. In contrast, an uncapped variable rate may start at nine percent, but with no ceiling, can rise to 20 percent or more as happened in the early 1980s. Variable rates are always dangerous but this type of rate leaves you without any protection whatsoever.

24) ***Non-interest bearing deposits.*** These deposits do draw interest—but not for you! Insist that if the terms of the contract are not satisfied by a certain date, any monies deposited by you will begin to earn interest at prevailing money market rates.

25) ***Food freezer plans.*** This plan has many interesting variations. Some sell you food with low monthly payments. Others force you to buy enormous quantities. Others only discount your opening order. And still others are not transferable outside your geographic area. These plans eagerly extend credit because they

all have one goal: To get you to buy the freezer at three to five times what you can buy a comparable freezer for at a local store. These plans are even more grateful if you lease the freezer, because at the end of the contract you must return the freezer. Be very careful with food plans. Read the fine print carefully. Do the math. Joining these plans is rarely a good deal from a credit viewpoint.

There are, of course, many other credit scams. And new ones are conceived daily. But how do you avoid them?

- Be patient
- Be suspicious
- Read the fine print
- Do not sign anything that you do not understand
- Check references
- Practice good credit management
- Avoid quick-fix solutions. If it sounds too good to be true, it probably is.

Key points to remember:

- If monthly payments are low, the interest rate is usually high.
- Always figure the total cost of your loan at the end of the loan period.
- Have all charges explained to you and put in writing.
- Be sure any merchandise you buy on credit is competitively priced.
- Be wary of deals that seem too good to be true.
- Do not be afraid to negotiate.
- Seek credit from those who report to the credit bureaus.

Glossary of Useful Terms

A-Ca

Accounts receivable

Any outstanding money owed to a business, usually by its customers, that is considered collectible.

Accounts receivable financing

Short-term financing based on outstanding accounts receivable.

Alert

One of a number of signals used by credit bureaus to indicate to creditors that there is a discrepancy in the credit report.

Applicant

The person who applies to a creditor for credit.

APR

Annual Percentage Rate. The annual cost of credit expressed as a percentage.

Assets

The resources, property or property rights owned by an individual or company.

Bankruptcy code

The body of federal statutory law that governs the bankruptcy process.

Balance

The amount owed on an account.

Cash advance

A loan obtained at a bank or ATM machine which is charged to a credit card.

Ce-Creditor

Certified mail

A postal service allowing you to obtain proof of delivery.

Chapter 7

The debtor's business is liquidated and its assets are distributed to creditors who have verifiable claims.

Chapter 11

A reorganization proceeding. The debtor continues to operate the business after bankruptcy is filed.

Chapter 13

Only filed by an individual debtor with limited debt. It allows a payment plan for an individual's personal or business debt.

Charge-off

A debt that is no longer considered to be collectable.

Collateral

Assets that are given as security for a loan.

Consolidation loan

One loan that is used to pay back a number of different loans.

Consumer statement

A statement of 100 words or less from a consumer explaining why he or she continues to dispute a credit report entry. This statement must be attached to, and sent out with the credit report.

Co-signer

Another person who applies for a loan and assumes equal liability for it.

Credit history

A record of what you have borrowed and repaid.

Credit scoring system

A statistical system used to evaluate an applicant's creditworthiness.

Creditor

One to whom you owe money.

Creditor Settlement Agreement

An agreement between creditor and debtor whereby the creditor agrees to remove negative entries from the debtor's credit report in exchange for full or partial repayment of the debt.

Credit-Fe

Creditworthiness

A creditor's evaluation of an applicant's past and future ability and willingness to repay debts.

Debit card

A card that deducts a transaction from an account such as a checking account.

Debtor

One who owes debts.

Default

Failure to meet the terms of a credit agreement.

Depreciation

Reduction in the book value of an asset. Depreciation can be deducted from taxable income.

Down payment

A part of the full price usually paid in cash, at the time of the purchase.

Equity

A company's net worth. Something of value.

Excessive inquiries

Too many credit inquiries in a short period of time make lenders become suspicious of a credit applicant's apparent sudden need for credit.

Factoring

A financial company's purchase of a firm's accounts receivable and the collection of those debts.

Fair Credit Reporting Act

A public law enacted to protect consumers from credit abuses.

Federal Deposit Insurance Corporation

A government agency that insures most commercial and savings bank accounts.

Federal Reserve System

The central bank for the United States.

Federal Trade Commission (FTC)

The government agency responsible for overseeing credit reporting practices.

Fi-M

File

All of the information that the credit bureau has on a consumer which is used to compile the credit report.

Finance charge

The total dollar amount paid to obtain a debt.

Foreclosure

A debt collection procedure whereby the property (often real estate) of the debtor is sold to satisfy debts.

Frivolous and irrelevant

A term applied by credit bureaus to consumer dispute letters that are suspected to be part of a plan to bombard the bureau with so much work that it can not meet deadlines.

Grace period

The period of time before the payment is due.

Inventory financing

Loans based upon the value of unsold inventory. The loan is repaid when the inventory is sold.

Joint account

An account that two or more people can use with each person assuming full responsibility to repay.

Lease

A long-term rental agreement.

Liability

A present obligation.

Late payment

Any payment made after the due date of the credit agreement.

Lien

An interest in Property securing the repayment of a debt.

Liquid assets

Assets most easily turned into cash.

Merged accounts

Two accounts are combined and become one entry.

Motion

A request for the court to act.

O-U

Obsolete information

Negative entries that remain on a credit report beyond the statutory time limit.

Pre-payment penalty

A fee paid by the borrower to the lender in the event that the loan is prepaid before it is due.

Public record information

Events that are a matter of public record and are related to your creditworthiness.

Regulatory agency

An agency that has the power to enforce laws.

Secured loans

Loans that are backed by collateral.

Unsecured loans

Loans that are not backed by collateral.

Sample Credit Reports

TYPICAL CREDIT REPORT

PERSONAL INFORMATION

John Q. Public
123 Your Street
Hometown, State Zip

Social Security Number: xxx-xx-xxx
Date of Birth: 01/00/2002

PREVIOUS ADDRESS(ES)

824 Some Avenue
That Place, State Zip

987 Main Place
Anywhere, State Zip

EMPLOYMENT DATA

Current Employment:
Employer's Name
Employer's Address

Employment Date:

Date Verified:

Previous Employment:
Employer's Name
Employer's Address

Employment Date:

Date Verified:

Previous Employment:
Employer's Name
Employer's Address

Employment Date:

Date Verified:

PUBLIC RECORDS DATA

This area lists information which is found as a matter of public record and is readily available to anyone. It includes items such as:

Bankruptcies on file
Liens on file
Judgements of file
Garnishments on file
Secured Loans on file
Marital Status on file
Financial Counsellings on file
Foreclosures on file
Non-responsibility Entities on file

COLLECTION ACCOUNTS

Accounts which have been or are presently in the collection process will appear listed in this area of your Credit Report.

CREDIT BACKGROUND

Information regarding credit cards, loans, revolving charge accounts, etc. will be enumerated in this area. For example:

Company	Account Owner and Number	Date Opened	Last Activity	Account Type and Status	Credit Limit	Balance Due	Past Due	Reported
Household Bank NA IL	70600-XXXXX-XXXX INDIVIDUAL ACCOUNT	08/1988	03/02	Revolving PAY AS AGREED	$10500		$0	03/0202

Prior Paying History
PAID ACCOUNT/ZERO BALANCE
CHARGE

Company	Account Owner and Number	Date Opened	Last Activity	Account Type and Status	Credit Limit	Balance Due	Past Due	Reported
Southtrust Bank	1000135XXXX CO-MAKER	10/1998		Unknown	$18290		$0	10/2001

Prior Paying History
30 days past due 00 times; 60 days past due 00 times; 90+days past due 00 times;
LEASE

CREDIT REQUEST HISTORY

Inquiries into your credit history or verification of your credit history will appear listed in this area of your Credit Report. For example:

03/20/01	AR	MBNA
03/30/01	PRM	Citibank
06/15/01	PRM	Nationwide Insurance
08/21/00		Chevy Chase Bank

PRM, AM and AR only appear on a Credit Report which you have requested.

PRM historically represent a promotional inquiry into your account where your name and address were submitted to a credit grantor for verification of credit for a promotional offering.

AM or AR historically represents a request for your credit history for a periodic review of your performance by an existing creditor (i.e. for increasing credit lines).

CONSUMER STATEMENTS

This area of your Credit Report displays your rebuttal to negative information contained in your Credit Report. For example:

I purchased faulty merchandise from XYZ department store just before that branch closed down. My letters to the company were never answered. When I finally reached a supervisor on the phone, he said too much time had elapsed and nothing could be done. I refused to continue paying on the account until a settlement was made. The company ignored my request and reported my account as a charge off. Even though I paid off the balance, they refuse to remove the charge off.

Dated_____

Signed_____

Sample Letters

21b. Creditor Settlement Agreement

21c. Creditor Settlement Agreement

22a. Consumer Statement

22b. Consumer Statement

22c. Consumer Statement

23. Request for Secondary Credit Card

24. Request for Investigative Report

25. Complaint to the Federal Trade Commission

26. Complaint to State Regulatory Agency

27. Complaint to Better Business Bureau

28. Complaint to Federal Deposit Insurance Corporation

29. Complaint to Comptroller of the Currency

30. Complaint to Federal Reserve System

Sample Letter No. 1a

Request for Credit Report
(not based upon credit denial)

Date:

Name of Credit Bureau
Address of Credit Bureau
City, State, Zip

To Whom It May Concern:

   Enclosed please find my check for $_____ to cover the indicated cost of providing me with a copy of my credit report. Please forward my current credit report as soon as possible to the name and address below:

Name:
Present Address:
Previous Address:
Social Security No.:
Date of Birth:
Employer Name:
Employer Address:
Spouse Name:

Sincerely yours,

Signature

Your Name

Sample Letter No. 1b

Request for Credit Report
(not based upon credit denial)

Date:

Name of Credit Bureau
Address of Credit Bureau
City, State, Zip

To Whom It May Concern:

Please send me a copy of my credit report.

My full name is:
My social security number is:
My date of birth is:
My current address is:
My previous address:
My employer is:
My employer's address is:
My spouse's name is:

Enclosed, please find my check (or money order) in the amount of $_____ to pay for the cost of the report. Please send the report to:

Yours truly,

Signature

Your Name

Sample Letter No. 2a

Request for Credit Report
(after credit denial)

Date:

Name of Credit Bureau
Address of Credit Bureau
City, State, Zip

To Whom It May Concern:

Please send me a copy of my credit report as soon as possible.

I have been denied credit within the past thirty days by

———,
based upon a credit report from your company. Enclosed please find a copy of the denial letter.

Name:
Present Address:
Previous Address:
Social Security No.:
Date of Birth:
Employer:
Employer Address:
Spouse's Name:

Your immediate attention to this matter is appreciated.

Very truly yours,

Signature

Your Name

Sample Letter No. 2b

Request for Credit Report
(after credit denial)

Date:

Name of Credit Bureau
Address of Credit Bureau
City, State, Zip

ATTN: Customer Relations Department

To Whom It May Concern:

Please mail me a free copy of my current credit report. Enclosed please find a copy of my denial letter.

Sincerely,

Signature

Your Name
Address
Social Security Number
Date of Birth
Previous Address
Spouse's Name
Employer's Name & Address

Sample Letter No. 3a

First Dispute Letter—General

Date:

Name of Credit Bureau
Address of Credit Bureau
City, State, Zip

To Whom It May Concern:

I formally request that the following inaccurate items be immediately investigated. They must be removed in order to show my true credit history, as these items should not be on my report. Pursuant to the Fair Credit Reporting Act, I will expect you to complete the verification within 30 (thirty) days.

Company Name	Account Number	Comments

Please send me my updated report as soon as your investigation is completed.

Sincerely,

Signature

Your Name
Address
Social Security Number
Date of Birth

Sample Letter No. 3b

First Dispute Letter—Late Payments

Date:

Name of Credit Bureau
Address of Credit Bureau
City, State, Zip

To Whom It May Concern:

My credit report lists the following accounts as reflecting late payments. These accounts are in error because they were paid on time. Please reinvestigate the following accounts and update my credit report to accurately reflect my credit history. Pursuant to the Fair Credit Reporting Act, I will expect you to complete the verification within 30 (thirty) days.

1)

2)

3)

4)

I would appreciate your sending me an updated copy of my file as soon as you have completed the investigation.

Sincerely,

Signature

Your Name
Address
Social Security Number
Date of Birth

Sample Letter No. 4

Second Dispute Letter—Remaining Items

Date:

Name of Credit Bureau
Address of Credit Bureau
City, State, Zip

To Whom It May Concern:

Thank you for deleting some of the accounts which incorrectly appeared on my credit report. However, I still vigorously dispute the following remaining items. These accounts are still being reported inaccurately and are extremely damaging to me.

In accordance with the Fair Credit Reporting Act Section 1681i, I ask that you reinvestigate these items and delete them from my report.

1)

2)

3)

Furthermore, I would appreciate the names of the individuals you contacted for verification, along with their addresses and phone numbers so I may follow up.

Sincerely,

Signature

Your Name
Address
Social Security Number
Date of Birth

Sample Letter No. 5a

Follow-Up Letter—Bureau Did Not Respond to Dispute Letter

Date:

Name of Credit Bureau
Address of Credit Bureau
City, State, Zip

To Whom It May Concern:

I am enclosing a copy of a letter that I mailed to you on (date) requesting that you verify the alleged debt your company claims I owe. The return receipt was signed on (date), copy enclosed. More than 30 days have passed and I have not yet received proof that you have validated the debt.

Therefore, in accordance with s.1692e(8) of the Debt Collection Practices Act, which clearly states that any information ". . . known to be false, or should be known to be false . . ." cannot be reported to any credit bureau, I request that you immediately delete this false and misleading information from my credit report.

Please send me a copy of my updated credit report as soon as the above has been completed.

Sincerely,

Signature

Your Name
Address
Social Security Number
Date of Birth

Sample Letter No. 5b

Follow-Up Letter—Bureau Did Not Respond to Dispute Letter

Date:

Name of Credit Bureau
Address of Credit Bureau
City, State, Zip

To Whom It May Concern:

On (date of first dispute letter), I sent you a request to investigate certain items on my credit report that I believe to be incorrect or inaccurate. But as of today, four weeks have passed and I have received no response from you.

Under the Fair Credit Reporting Act, you are obligated to respond within 30 (thirty) days. Since the information cannot be verified, please delete it from my credit report.

I would appreciate your immediate attention to this matter. Please send me a copy of my updated report.

Sincerely,

Signature

Your Name
Address
Social Security Number
Date of Birth

Sample Letter No. 5c

Follow-Up Letter—Bureau Did Not Respond to Dispute Letter

Date:

Name of Credit Bureau
Address of Credit Bureau
City, State, Zip

To Whom It May Concern:

Four weeks ago, I sent you a second letter reminding you that you had not responded to or investigated disputed and incorrect items on my credit report. Copies of that letter and the original dispute letter are enclosed. This is the third letter I am sending you regarding my initial disputes.

The Fair Credit Reporting Act requires your company to ensure the correctness of reported information. To date, you still have not compiled with your obligation. I therefore demand that you immediately remove the disputed items from my credit report because they are either inaccurate or cannot be verified. I also expect you to send me an updated copy of my credit report as soon as this is completed.

If I do not receive your response within the next 15 days, I will file a complaint with the Federal Trade Commission, the subcommittee on Banking and Finance and the Attorney General of (the state in which the credit bureau is located).

Sincerely,

Signature

Your Name
Address
Social Security Number
Date of Birth

Sample Letter No. 5d

Follow-Up Letter—Bureau Did Not Respond to Dispute Letter

Date:

Name of Credit Bureau
Address of Credit Bureau
City, State, Zip

To Whom It May Concern:

On (date) I wrote to your company about serious and inaccurate information in my credit report. You received this letter on (date), as evidenced by the certified mail receipt.

In my (date of first letter) letter, I asked you to respond to my request within 30 days, as per 15 U.S.C. § 1681i(a)(1)(A). Because I have not received a reply from you within this 30-day period, I must assume that the disputed information was either inaccurate or you were unable to reverify the information. You must now comply with the law and "promptly delete such information" from my credit report.

Please respond immediately, as I will not hesitate to pursue this matter further. I will take full advantage of my rights under the Fair Credit Reporting Act if you fail to comply, and I will file a complaint with the Federal Trade Commission and the subcommittee on Banking and Finance.

Sincerely,

Signature

Your Name
Address
Social Security Number
Date of Birth

Sample Letter No. 6a

Dispute of Unauthorized Credit
Inquiry—To Creditor

Date:

Name of Creditor
Address of Creditor
City, State, Zip

To Whom It May Concern:

I have been informed that your company, on (date of inquiry) ran an unauthorized credit report on me. At no time did I ever authorize you to do this. This action on your part constitutes a violation of my rights under the Fair Credit Reporting Act. This is illegal and highly injurious to my credit rating.

Unless you immediately contact the credit bureau and remove this inquiry from my report, I will have no choice but to take legal action.

Please govern yourself accordingly.

Sincerely,

Signature

Your Name
Address
Social Security Number
Date of Birth

Sample Letter No. 6b

Dispute of Unauthorized Credit Inquiry—To Bureau

Date:

Name of Credit Bureau
Address of Credit Bureau
City, State, Zip

To Whom It May Concern:

At the earliest opportunity, please provide me with the names, addresses and phone numbers of the following subscribers:

Subscriber Name	Subscriber No.	Date
1.		
2.		
3.		
4.		

According to my credit report (see attached copy), these subscribers have run unauthorized credit reports on me. I wish to contact them to find out why.

Your immediate attention to this matter is greatly appreciated.

Sincerely,

Signature

Your Name
Address
Social Security Number
Date of Birth

Sample Letter No. 6c

Dispute of Unauthorized Credit
Inquiry—To Bureau

Date:

Name of Credit Bureau
Address of Credit Bureau
City, State, Zip

To Whom It May Concern:

The following inquiries were not authorized by me, please delete them. Never having given my permission for them to inquire about my credit status, they are unauthorized by me. Their continued presence on my credit report constitutes inaccurate information, which, under the Fair Credit Reporting Act, must be removed.

1)
2)
3)
4)

Furthermore, I would appreciate the names, addresses and phone numbers of these companies so I may follow up.

Sincerely,

Signature

Your Name
Address
Social Security Number
Date of Birth

Sample Letter No. 7a

Request for Removal of Outdated Information

Date:

Name of Credit Bureau
Address of Credit Bureau
City, State, Zip

To Whom It May Concern:

Please note that under Section 1681c of the Federal Fair Credit Reporting Act you are obligated to delete obsolete information from the consumer credit report of the undersigned.

Please refer to the information circled on the attached copy of the consumer credit report. It is obsolete and should be deleted immediately from your credit files relating to the undersigned.

I anticipate your immediate attention to this matter.

Sincerely,

Signature

Your Name
Address
Social Security Number
Date of Birth

Sample Letter No. 7b

Request for Removal of Outdated Information

Date:

Name of Credit Bureau
Address of Credit Bureau
City, State, Zip

To Whom It May Concern:

I have received my current credit report and I need to bring to your attention several entries that are outdated.

1)

2)

3)

Since these entries are more than seven years old and exceed the statutory time period under the Fair Credit Reporting Act, they must be removed. Please send my updated/revised credit report to me after these have been deleted.

Your prompt attention to this matter is greatly appreciated.

Sincerely,

Signature

Your Name
Address
Social Security Number
Date of Birth

Sample Letter No. 8

Request to Remove Bankruptcy Information

Date:

Name of Credit Bureau
Address of Credit Bureau
City, State, Zip

To Whom It May Concern:

I appreciate the removal of most of the accounts listed in my letter dated (date). I am disturbed, however, that you continue to list the dismissed (filed) bankruptcy as confirmed. Although it is your policy to keep reporting bankruptcies which are filed, dismissed or adjudicated for ten years, the Fair Credit Reporting Act mentions nothing in Section 1681c relating to bankruptcy about dismissals or filings. The law clearly states from "date of adjudication" or date of "order for relief".

Any case, civil or otherwise, which is dismissed no longer exists in the eyes of the law and a case filed may never have actually been adjudicated. Therefore, you have no right to maintain information which the government has deemed nonexistent.

Therefore, it is only fair that in accordance with Section 1681(a)(5) of the FCRA you delete this from my credit report and send me an updated copy when it is completed.

Considering that this does not require an investigation, I would appreciate your response within two weeks from the date you receive this letter.

Sincerely,

Signature

Your Name
Address
Social Security Number
Date of Birth

Sample Letter No. 9a

Challenge to Verification Process

Date:

Name of Credit Bureau
Address of Credit Bureau
City, State, Zip

To Whom It May Concern:

In accordance with the law, I have sent a letter (copy attached) to the following creditors in order to verify the debts you allege that I owe. Since these creditors cannot verify these debts to me, even though I am the alleged debtor, how can your bureau claim to have verified them? As you can see, these were sent certified mail return receipt requested.

Since these debts have not been verified according to the law, I demand that you remove all reference to these accounts from my credit report within the next 30 days.

Sincerely,

Signature

Your Name
Address
Social Security Number
Date of Birth

Sample Letter No. 9b

Challenge to Verification Process

Date:

Name of Collection Agency
Address of Collection Agency
City, State, Zip

To Whom It May Concern:

I have received a letter claiming that I owe a debt to (name). Since this is in error, I request that you send me the following proofs as you are obligated to do in accordance with the Debt Collection Practices Act, Section 1692g.

1)   The original application or contract

2)   Any and all statements allegedly related to this debt

3)   Any and all signed receipts

4)   Any and all canceled checks

Under the law, you have 30 days to supply these proofs. In addition, do not contact me again in any way. From now on, we will communicate through the mail.

Sincerely,

Signature

Your Name
Address
Social Security Number
Date of Birth

Sample Letter No. 10

Request to Remove Checkpoints, Alerts and File Variations

Date:

Name of Credit Bureau
Address of Credit Bureau
City, State, Zip

To Whom It May Concern:

Please remove the following checkpoints, alerts and file variations which are being maintained incorrectly on my credit report. Obviously, these are typos or errors and make my credit report appear as though I am engaged in fraud.

The only information that should appear on my report is the correction information listed on this letter. Please make these corrections and send me a copy of my updated report for my files.

1)
2)
3)

Furthermore, please provide me with the names, addresses and phone numbers of the companies who caused these errors so I may follow up.

Sincerely,

Signature

Your Name
Address
Social Security Number
Date of Birth

Sample Letter No. 11

Response to Frivolous and Irrelevant

Date:

Name of Credit Bureau
Address of Credit Bureau
City, State, Zip

To Whom It May Concern:

I am in receipt of your illegal letter dated (date) claiming that my dispute is "frivolous and irrelevant." Of course, you have no way of knowing that because thus far you have not fulfilled your obligation under the law and re-investigated it.

I have forwarded a copy of this illegal letter to the Federal Trade Commission and to the subcommittee on Banking, Credit and Insurance.

I fully expect that you will fulfill your legal obligation and re-investigate the items contained in my letter dated (date) and sent to you certified mail, return receipt requested.

I will follow up with a phone call to confirm when you will begin the work and when you will be completed.

Sincerely,

Signature

Your Name
Address
Social Security Number
Date of Birth

Sample Letter No. 12

Response to Credit Repair Service

Date:

Name of Credit Bureau
Address of Credit Bureau
City, State, Zip

To Whom It May Concern:

In response to your illegal letter dated (date), stating that you are under no obligation to investigate the disputed entries that I had listed in my letter to you dated (date) sent return receipt requested (copy enclosed), because in your opinion I am using a "credit repair service," I am claiming that you are mistaken on two counts:

1.   The FCRA obligates you to investigate any disputed claim within 30 days. The FCRA does not provide you with an exception for credit repair service intervention. So far, you have not fulfilled your obligation to do so and are in clear violation of the law.

2.   I am not now using, nor have I ever used a credit repair service. I have no need to because I am familiar with the law and am prepared to take full advantage of the protection it affords me. There is much information published by the Federal Trade Commission's Bureau of Consumer Protection in Washington, D.C. I refer specifically to publications F008698, 6002, F002472, and F030508 in addition to the Fair Credit Reporting Act, which is a public document.

Therefore, I have a right to expect you to begin and complete the verification process within 30 (thirty) days from your receipt of this letter. If I do not receive confirmation of this within that time, I will forward a copy of all correspondence together with a formal complaint to the Federal Trade Commission and the subcommittee on Banking and Finance, in addition to numerous state consumer protection agencies.

Sincerely,

Signature
Your Name
Address
Social Security Number
Date of Birth

Sample Letter No. 13

Request for Personal Interview

Date:

Name of Credit Bureau
Address of Credit Bureau
City, State, Zip

To Whom It May Concern:

According to Sections 1681h(b)(2)(A) of the Federal Fair Credit Reporting Act, the undersigned is entitled to a personal interview with your bureau to obtain a copy of the consumer credit report issued by you and to review your files pertaining to the undersigned.

Therefore, the undersigned will appear at your office on (date) at (time) a.m./p.m. If this date or time is inconvenient, please advise so that a mutually agreeable date and/or time may be arranged.

Within the last thirty (30) days, the undersigned has received notice of credit denial wholly or partly as a result of a credit report from your bureau.

Accordingly, a fee is not due to your organization. Enclosed please find a copy of the denial letter. Please have the files of the undersigned ready for review.

Sincerely,

Signature

Your Name
Address
Social Security Number
Date of Birth

Sample Letter No. 14a

Request to Add Positive Information

Date:

Name of Credit Bureau
Address of Credit Bureau
City, State, Zip

To Whom It May Concern:

After reviewing my recent credit report from your company, I am dismayed to find that you do not list the following credit accounts. Please add this information to my credit report immediately.

If there is any fee for this service, please advise.

> Creditor
> Address
> Type of Account
> Account Number
> Date Opened
> Credit Limit
> Balance

Your cooperation in this matter is greatly appreciated.

Sincerely,

Signature

Your Name
Address
Social Security Number
Date of Birth

Sample Letter No. 14b

Request to Add Positive Information

Date:

Name of Credit Bureau
Address of Credit Bureau
City, State, Zip

To Whom It May Concern:

I would like you to please list the following credit references on my credit report.

Creditor's Name   Creditor's Address   Account Number

Please send me an updated credit report as soon as the above has been added. If there is any fee for adding this information, please advise.

Thank you for your assistance in this matter.

Sincerely,

Signature

Your Name
Address
Social Security Number
Date of Birth

Sample Letter No. 14c

Request to Add Positive Information

Date:

Name of Credit Bureau
Address of Credit Bureau
City, State, Zip

To Whom It May Concern:

In reviewing the credit file you maintain on me, I have discovered that my credit record fails to include information that I know is important to providing a complete portrait of me as a credit-using consumer. I therefore request that you add the following information to my credit report:

> Creditor
> Creditor's Address
> Account Number
> Account Type
>
> Creditor
> Creditor's Address
> Account Number
> Account Type

If you need additional information from me, I can be reached at (area code/telephone number and mailing address). Please let me know if there is a fee for this service.

Thank you for your attention to this matter.

Sincerely,

Signature

Your Name
Address
Social Security Number
Date of Birth

Sample Letter No. 15

Request for Husband and Wife File Separation

Date:

Name of Creditor
Address of Creditor
City, State, Zip

To Whom It May Concern:

Current Account Number:

Under the Equal Opportunity Act, a husband and wife are allowed to maintain separate files pertaining to credit information.

The undersigned request that credit information on the accounts of the undersigned be maintained in separate files.

We further request that all past, current and future information be reported as separate account information to all credit reporting agencies.

Sincerely,

Husband's Signature

Husband's Name

Wife's Signature

Wife's Name

Address

Sample Letter No. 16

Request to Merge Husband's and Wife's Accounts

Date:

Name of Creditor
Address of Creditor
City, State, Zip

To Whom It May Concern:

We request all information concerning the accounts listed below be reported as one account as provided for by the Equal Credit Opportunity Act, Regulation B.

> Name
> Spouse's Name
> Current Account Name
> Account Number

Sincerely,

Signature of Either Spouse

Name

Address

Sample Letter No. 17

Letter to Creditor Requesting Information Correction

Date:

Name of Creditor
Address of Creditor
City, State, Zip

Dear Credit Manager:

Recently I received a copy of my credit report from (name of credit bureau). Upon reviewing the report, I was dismayed to discover a problem relating to my account with you. My account number is _____.

The problem is (describe the problem as clearly and succinctly as possible).

Enclosed please find documentation that supports my case.

Please investigate this problem and notify me of your findings. If the information you have reported has not been accurate and complete, please provide the correct information to those credit bureaus you work with and direct them to make the appropriate changes in my files.

In addition, please send to me a copy of the information you send the credit bureaus in response to this letter. Please send that information to me at (mailing address).

I can be reached at (phone number).

Your prompt attention to this request is greatly appreciated.

Sincerely,

Signature
Your Name
Address
Account Number

Sample Letter No. 18

Letter to Creditor Disputing Wife's Account

Date:

Name of Creditor
Address of Creditor
City, State, Zip

Re: Account Number

To Whom It May Concern:

After carefully examining my current credit bureau reports, it has come to my attention that your company has mistakenly recorded the payment history/liability for the account referenced above.

This account belongs to my ex-wife, (name), and is solely her responsibility. We have been divorced for the last (number of years) and I am not responsible for this account.

According to the Fair Credit Reporting Act, you have 30 days from the date of receipt of this letter to remove all information from all credit bureaus you have reported this inaccurate information to, or send me written proof that I have ever signed documentation taking responsibility for this account.

I anticipate your prompt response.

Sincerely,

Signature

Your Name
Address
Social Security Number
Date of Birth

Sample Letter No. 19

Letter to Creditor Requesting Reasons for Credit Denial

Date:

Name of Creditor
Address of Creditor
City, State, Zip

To Whom It May Concern:

Recently, the undersigned was denied credit by your company.

Please be advised that pursuant to Section 1681m(b) of the Federal Fair Credit Reporting Act, the undersigned hereby requests a full disclosure of the factual information disclosed to you by persons other than Consumer Reporting Agencies concerning the undersigned. Such information must be in sufficient detail to allow the undersigned to refute, challenge or dispute its accuracy.

Please take further notice that you are required to render such notification to the undersigned within thirty (30) days as per the FCRA.

Sincerely,

Signature

Your Name
Address
City, State, Zip

Sample Letter No. 20

Request That Creditors Receive Updated Report

Date:

Name of Credit Bureau
Address of Credit Bureau
City, State, Zip

To Whom It May Concern:

Pursuant to Section 1681i(d) of the Federal Fair Credit Reporting Act, the undersigned hereby requests that you notify every person who has received the deleted or disputed information within the past two (2) years and notify them that such information has been subsequently deleted.

If there is any fee for this service, please notify me immediately.

Sincerely,

Signature

Your Name
Address
Social Security Number
Date of Birth

Sample Letter No. 21a

Creditor Settlement Agreement

Date:

Name of Creditor
Address of Creditor
City, State, Zip

Re: Account Number

Dear   :

This letter is to confirm our telephone conversation on (date) regarding the settlement of the above account.

As discussed, I will pay your company the amount of $_____ as full settlement of this account.

Upon receipt of the above consideration, your company has agreed to change the entry on my credit file to "paid satisfactory." In addition, any adverse credit information regarding my account, such as "late payment" or "charge off" should be deleted from my report.

If you agree to the aforementioned terms and conditions, please acknowledge with your signature and return a copy to me. Upon receipt of this signed acknowledgment, I will immediately forward you a cashier's check in the amount stated above.

_____
Signature of Authorized Officer

_____
Date

_____
Name

_____
Title

Sincerely,

Signature

Your Name

Address

Sample Letter No. 21b

Creditor Settlement Agreement

Date:

Name of Creditor
Address of Creditor
City, State, Zip

Gentlemen:

I am writing to confirm our agreement regarding the settlement of a debt that I previously owed to your company. The terms I propose are as follows:

1. "I," (your name), agree to pay (creditor's name) ("You") $(dollar amount) in full satisfaction of all amounts that I owe to You and You agree to accept $(dollar amount) from me in full satisfaction of all amounts that I previously owed to You.

2. I agree to pay the $(dollar amount) in (number) monthly installments of $(dollar amount), without interest. The first payment to begin on (date) and each remaining payment on the (day) of each following month. I will mail these payments to your office, located at (address).

3. If I do not pay the full amount of each payment when it is due, I will be in default. If I am in default, You may send me a written notice telling me that if I do not pay the overdue amount by a certain date, the entire unpaid balance will be due within 30 days after the date on which the notice is delivered or mailed to me.

4. Upon discharging this debt, you agree to notify each credit bureau to which You report credit information that any adverse credit information regarding my account with You is no longer verifiable and should be deleted from my credit report.

If You agree to the foregoing terms and conditions, please sign the Agreement and the enclosed copy in the places provided and return the documents to me.

Date:

Accepted and Agreed	Signature
By:_____	Your Name
Name	Address
Title	Account Number

Sample Letter No. 21c

Creditor Settlement Agreement

Date:

Name of Creditor
Address of Creditor
City, State, Zip

Dear Name of Creditor:

As a result of an illness, I am unemployed and unable to pay my debt to your company. My lack of income leaves nothing for such payments. It is impossible for me to raise enough money to satisfy you or other creditors since I have nothing of value to sell.

I am willing, however, to offer you a settlement of (number) cents on the dollar as payment in full for this obligation. Since my balance with your company is $(dollar amount), I am willing to send you $(dollar amount) as payment in full next (day), after I cash my last paycheck.

If you are willing to accept this offer, please sign and return this letter to me as soon as possible.

Sincerely,

Signature

Your Name
Address
Account Number

Accepted by:

_____
Signature   Date
Name:_____
Title: _____

Sample Letter No. 22a

Consumer Statement

Date:

Name of Credit Bureau
Address of Credit Bureau
City, State, Zip

To Whom It May Concern:

Having sent you a letter disputing incorrect information on my credit report regarding one of my creditors and having received notification from you that you would not alter the reported information, I now demand that you include the following consumer statement in my credit report:

Pursuant to the Fair Credit Reporting Act, Section 1681i(a)(5)(B)(iii)(III), you are obligated to include my statement in any subsequent consumer report that includes the disputed information. Furthermore, because my statement contains less than 100 words, I demand that you include the full text of the statement in my report, without changes, alterations or summaries.

Please send me a copy of my updated credit report once the above has been completed.

Please give this matter your immediate attention.

Sincerely,

Signature

Your Name
Address
Social Security Number
Date of Birth

Sample Letter No. 22b

Consumer Statement

Date:

Name of Credit Bureau
Address of Credit Bureau
City, State, Zip

To Whom It May Concern:

Pursuant to 15 U.S.C. § 1681i(b), I request the following consumer statement be included in my credit report:

Please forward me a copy of my updated credit report as soon as the above has been completed.

Sincerely,

Signature

Your Name
Address
Social Security Number
Date of Birth

Sample Letter No. 22c

Consumer Statement

Date:

Name of Credit Bureau
Address of Credit Bureau
City, State, Zip

To Whom It May Concern:

I refer to the following inaccurate information presently maintained in your files concerning the undersigned:

> Creditor
> Item
> Amount of alleged debt

Please be advised that the undersigned vigorously disputes the truth of such information and demands the following consumer statement be included in any subsequent credit reports:

The undersigned does not owe the account and disputes the charge for the following reasons:

Pursuant to 15 U.S.C. § 1681i(b) of the Federal Fair Credit Reporting Act, you are obligated to update your records to include a copy of such consumer statement or a clear and accurate summary of such.

Sincerely,

Signature

Your Name
Address
Social Security Number
Date of Birth

Sample Letter No. 23

Request for Secondary Credit Card

Date:

Name of Bank/Department Store
Credit Card Department
Address of Bank/Department Store
City, State, Zip

To Whom It May Concern:

I, (name of primary cardholder), as primary credit-card holder, request that a secondary card be issued to the following person. I will guarantee the payment on this account.

> Name of Secondary Card Applicant
> Address of Secondary Card Applicant
> Social Security Number of Secondary Card Applicant
> Date of Birth of Secondary Card Applicant

Thank you for your cooperation. Your immediate attention to this matter is greatly appreciated.

Sincerely,

Signature

Your Name
Address
Account Number

Sample Letter No. 24

Request for Investigative Report

Date:

Name of Creditor
Address of Creditor
City, State, Zip

To Whom It May Concern:

I have been informed that a request for an investigative consumer report concerning me was recently made by your company.

Please be advised that, pursuant to Section 1681d(b) of the Federal Fair Credit Reporting Act which requires a response by you within five (5) days, a request is hereby made by me for a complete and accurate disclosure of the nature and source of the investigation on me.

Sincerely,

Signature

Your Name
Address

Sample Letter No. 25

Complaint to the Federal Trade Commission

Date:

Federal Trade Commission
6th & Pennsylvania Avenue, NW
Washington, DC 20580

Dear Sirs:

I understand that you have enforcement powers against credit bureaus under 15 U.S.C. §1681s. Therefore, I wish to lodge a complaint with you so that you may be aware of and able to act upon a matter of abuse of that Consumer Reporting Act.

> Name of Credit Bureau
> Address of Credit Bureau

This credit bureau has refused to comply with its obligations under the Fair Credit Reporting Act. The substance of my complaint is as follows:

Please investigate this matter and inform me of the results. The undersigned would be happy to furnish full particulars to you if you need further information for enforcement proceedings.

Sincerely,

Signature

Your Name
Address

Sample Letter No. 26

Complaint to State Regulatory Agency

Date:

Name of Your State's Agency
Address
City, State Zip

Dear Sirs:

I wish to lodge a complaint with you against the following credit bureau for engaging in illegal and unfair business practices. This credit bureau has refused to comply with its obligations under the Federal Fair Credit Reporting Act.

> Name of Credit Bureau
> Address of Credit Bureau

Your organization is hereby notified of such complaint so that you may be aware of a pattern of abuse and that you may take enforcement proceedings.

The substance of my complaint is as follows:

Please investigate this matter and inform me of the results. For your convenience, I have attached copies of all correspondence. Thank you in advance for your assistance in this matter.

Sincerely,

Signature

Your Name
Address

Sample Letter No. 27

Complaint to Better Business Bureau

Date:

Better Business Bureau
Address
City, State Zip

To Whom It May Concern:

I, (your name), hereby lodge a complaint against the following credit reporting bureau:

> Name of Credit Bureau
> Address of Credit Bureau

This credit reporting bureau has refused to comply with its obligations under the Federal Fair Credit Reporting Act. The substance of the complaint is as follows:

Your organization is hereby notified of such complaint so that (a) you may be aware of a pattern of abuse, and (b) you may take action to help consumers.

The undersigned would be happy to furnish any additional information you may need.

Sincerely,

Signature

Your Name
Address

Sample Letter No. 28

Complaint to Federal Deposit Insurance Corporation

Date:

Federal Deposit Insurance Corporation
Office of Bank Customer Affairs
Washington DC 20429

Re: Name of Bank
       Address
       City, State Zip
       Account Number (if applicable)

To Whom It May Concern:

I wish to file a formal complaint on the above referenced bank. My complaint is as follows:

I have tried unsuccessfully to resolve the above-described problem directly with (name of bank). The key person I dealt with was (name of bank employee).

I have enclosed photocopies of all pertinent paperwork and correspondence to document my claims.

Sincerely,

Signature

Your Name
Address

Sample Letter No. 29

Complaint to Comptroller of the Currency

Date:

Comptroller of the Currency
Consumer Affairs Division
Washington DC 20219

Re: Name of Bank
       Address
       City, State Zip
       Account Number (if applicable)

To Whom It May Concern:

I wish to file a formal complaint on the above referenced bank. My complaint is as follows:

I have tried unsuccessfully to resolve the above-described problem directly with (name of bank). The key person I dealt with was (name of bank employee).

I have enclosed photocopies of all pertinent paperwork and correspondence to document my claims.

Sincerely,

Signature

Your Name
Address

Sample Letter No. 30

Complaint to Federal Reserve System

Date:

Director, Division of Consumer Affairs
Board of Governor of the
Federal Reserve System
Washington DC 20551

Re: Name of Bank
        Address
        City, State Zip
        Account Number (if applicable)

To Whom It May Concern:

I wish to file a formal complaint on the above referenced bank. My complaint is as follows:

I have tried unsuccessfully to resolve the above-described problem directly with (name of bank). The key person I dealt with was (name of bank employee).

I have enclosed photocopies of all pertinent paperwork and correspondence to document my claims.

Sincerely,

Signature

Your Name
Address

Fair Credit Reporting Act

THE FAIR CREDIT REPORTING ACT

UNITED STATES CODE ANNOTATED
TITLE 15. COMMERCE AND TRADE
CHAPTER 41—CONSUMER CREDIT PROTECTION
SUBCHAPTER III—CREDIT REPORTING AGENCIES
Current through P.L. 103-251, approved 5-16-94

§ 1681. Congressional findings and statement of purpose

(a) The Congress makes the following findings:

(1) The banking system is dependent upon fair and accurate credit reporting. Inaccurate credit reports directly impair the efficiency of the banking system, and unfair credit reporting methods undermine the public confidence which is essential to the continued functioning of the banking system.

(2) An elaborate mechanism has been developed for investigating and evaluating the credit worthiness, credit standing, credit capacity, character, and general reputation of consumers.

(3) Consumer reporting agencies have assumed a vital role in assembling and evaluating consumer credit and other information on consumers.

(4) There is a need to insure that consumer reporting agencies exercise their grave responsibilities with fairness, impartiality, and a respect for the consumer's right to privacy.

(b) It is the purpose of this subchapter to require that consumer reporting agencies adopt reasonable procedures for meeting the needs of commerce for consumer credit, personnel, insurance, and other information in a manner which is fair and equitable to the consumer, with regard to the confidentiality, accuracy, relevancy, and proper utilization of such information in accordance with the requirements of this subchapter.

§ 1681a. Definitions; rules of construction

(a) Definitions and rules of construction set forth in this section are applicable for the purposes of this subchapter.

(b) The term "person" means any individual, partnership, corporation, trust, estate, cooperative, association, government or governmental subdivision or agency, or other entity.

(c) The term "consumer" means an individual.

(d) Consumer report.

(1) In general. The term means any written, oral, or other

communication of any information by a consumer reporting agency bearing on a consumer's credit worthiness, credit standing, credit capacity, character, general reputation, personal characteristics, or mode of living which is used or expected to be used or collected in whole or in part for the purpose of serving as a factor in establishing the consumer's eligibility for

(A) credit or insurance to be used primarily for personal, family, or household purposes;

(B) employment purposes; or

(C) any other purpose authorized under section 1681b of this title.

(2) Exclusions. The term "consumer report" does not include

(A) Any

(i) report containing information solely as to transactions or experiences between the consumer and the person making the report;

(ii) communication of that information among persons related by common ownership or affiliated by corporate control;

(iii) any communication of that information among persons related by common ownership or affiliated by corporate control, if it is clearly and conspicuously disclosed to the consumer that the information may be communicated among such persons and the consumer is given the opportunity, before the time that the information is initially communicated, to direct that such information not be communicated among such persons;

(B) any authorization or approval of a specific extension of credit directly or indirectly by the issuer of a credit card or similar device; or

(C) any report in which a person who has been requested by a third party to make a specific extension of credit directly or indirectly to a consumer conveys his decision with respect to such request, if the third party advises the consumer of the name and address of the person to whom the request was made and such person makes the disclosures to the consumer required under section 1681m of this title; or

(D) a communication described in subsection (o) of this section.

(e) The term "investigative consumer report" means a consumer report or portion thereof in which information on a consumer's character, general reputation, personal characteristics, or mode of living is obtained through personal interviews with neighbors, friends, or associates of the consumer reported on or with others with whom he is acquainted or who may have knowledge concerning any such items of information. However, such information shall not include specific factual information on a consumer's credit record obtained directly from a creditor of the consumer or from a consumer reporting agency when such information was obtained directly from a creditor of the consumer or from the consumer.

(f) The term "consumer reporting agency" means any person which, for monetary fees, dues, or on a cooperative nonprofit basis, regularly engages in whole or in part in the practice of assembling or evaluating consumer credit information or other information on consumers for the purpose of furnishing consumer reports to third parties, and which uses any means or facility of interstate commerce for the purpose of preparing or furnishing consumer reports.

(g) The term "file", when used in connection with information on any consumer, means all of the information on that consumer recorded and retained by a consumer reporting agency regardless of how the information is stored.

(h) The term "employment purposes" when used in connection with a consumer report means a report used for the purpose of evaluating a consumer for employment, promotion, reassignment or retention as an employee.

(i) The term "medical information" means information or records obtained, with the consent of the individual to whom it relates, from licensed physicians or medical practitioners, hospitals, clinics, or other medical or medically related facilities.

(j) Definitions relating to child support obligations

    (1) Overdue support

        The term "overdue support" has the meaning given to such term in section 666(e) of Title 42.

    (2) State or local child support enforcement agency

        The term "State or local child support enforcement agency" means a State or local agency which administers a State or local program for establishing and enforcing child support obligations.

(k) Adverse action.

    (1) Actions included. The term "adverse action"

        (A) has the same meaning as in section 1691(d)(6) of this title; and

        (B) means

            (i) a denial or cancellation of, an increase in any charge for, or a reduction or other adverse or unfavorable change in the terms of coverage or amount of, any insurance, existing or applied for, in connection with the underwriting of insurance;

            (ii) a denial of employment of any other decision for employment purposes that adversely affects any current or prospective employee;

(iii) a denial or cancellation of, an increase in any charge for, or any other adverse or unfavorable change in the terms of, any license or benefit described in section 1681b (a)(3)(D) of this title; and

(iv) an action taken or determination that is

(I) made in connection with an application that was made by, or a transaction that was initiated by, any consumer, or in connection with a review of an account under section 1681b(a)(3)(F)(ii) of this title; and

(II) adverse to the interests of the consumer.

(2) Applicable findings, decisions, commentary, and orders.

For purposes of any determination of whether an action is an adverse action under paragraph (1)(A), all appropriate final findings, decisions, commentary, and orders issued under section 1691(d)(6) of this title by the Board of Governors of the Federal Reserve System or any court shall apply.

(l) Firm offer of credit or insurance.

The term "firm offer of credit or insurance" means any offer of credit or insurance to a consumer that will be honored if the consumer is determined, based on information in a consumer report on the consumer, to meet the specific criteria used to select the consumer for that offer, except that the offer may be further conditioned on one or more of the following:

(1) The consumer being determined, based on information in the consumer's application for the credit or insurance, to meet specific criteria bearing on credit worthiness or insurability, as applicable, that are established

(A) before selection of the consumer for the offer; and

(B) for the purpose of determining whether to extend credit or insurance pursuant to the offer.

(2) Verification

(A) that the consumer continues to meet the specific criteria used to select the consumer for the offer, by using information in a consumer report on the consumer, information in the consumer's application for the credit or insurance, or other information bearing on the credit worthiness or insurability of the consumer; or

(B) of the information in the consumer's application for the credit or insurance, to determine that the consumer meets the specific criteria bearing on credit worthiness or insurability.

(3) The consumer furnishing any collateral that is a requirement for the extension of the credit or insurance that was

(A) established before selection of the consumer for the offer of credit or insurance; and

(B) disclosed to the consumer in the offer of credit or insurance.

(m) Credit or insurance transaction that is not initiated by the consumer.

The term "credit or insurance transaction that is not initiated by the consumer" does not include the use of a consumer report by a person with which the consumer has an account or insurance policy, for purposes of

(1) reviewing the account or insurance policy; or

(2) collecting the account.

(n) State.

The term "state" means any State, the Commonwealth of Puerto Rico, the District of Columbia, and any territory or possession of the United States.

(o) Excluded communications.

A communication is described in this subsection if it is a communication

(1) that, but for subsection (d)(2)(E) of this section, would be an investigative consumer report;

(2) that is made to a prospective employer for the purpose of

(A) procuring an employee for the employer; or

(B) procuring an opportunity for a natural person to work for the employer;

(3) that is made by a person who regularly performs such procurement;

(4) that is not used by any person for any purpose other than a purpose described in subparagraph (A) or (B) of paragraph (2); or

(5) with respect to which

(A) the consumer who is the subject of the communication

(i) consents orally or in writing to the nature and scope of the communication, before the collection of any information for the purpose of making the communication;

(ii) consents orally or in writing to the making of the communication to a prospective employer, before making of the communication; and

(iii) in the case of consent under clause (i) or (ii) given orally, is provided written confirmation of that consent by the person making the communication, not later than 3 business days after the receipt of the consent by that person;

(B) the person who makes the communication does not, for the purpose of making the communication, make any inquiry that if made by a prospective employer of the consumer who is the subject of the communication would violate any applicable Federal or State equal employment opportunity law or regulation; and

(C) the person who makes the communication

    (i) discloses in writing to the consumer who is the subject of the communication, not later than 5 business days after receiving any request from the consumer for such disclosure, the nature and substance of all information in the consumer's file at the time of the request, except that the sources of any information that is acquired solely for use in making the communication and is actually used for no other purpose, need not be disclosed other than under appropriate discovery procedures in any court of competent jurisdiction in which an action is brought; and

    (ii) notifies the consumer who is the subject of the communication, in writing, of the consumer's right to request the information described in clause (i).

(p) Consumer reporting agency that compiles and maintains files on consumers on a nationwide basis.

The term "consumer reporting agency that compiles and maintains files on consumers on a nationwide basis" means a consumer reporting agency that regularly engages in the practice of assembling or evaluating, and maintaining, for the purpose of furnishing consumer reports to third parties bearing on a consumer's credit worthiness, credit standing, or credit capacity, each of the following regarding consumers residing nationwide:

(1) Public record information.

(2) Credit account information from persons who furnish that information regularly and in the ordinary course of business.

§ 1681b. Permissible purposes of consumer reports

(a) In general.

Subject to subsections (c) of this section, any consumer reporting agency may furnish a consumer report under the following circumstances and no other:

(1) In response to the order of a court having jurisdiction to issue such an order, or a subpoena issued in connection with proceedings before a Federal grand jury.

(2) In accordance with the written instructions of the consumer to whom it relates.

(3) To a person which it has reason to believe—

    (A) intends to use the information in connection with a credit transaction involving the consumer on whom the information is to be furnished and involving the extension of credit to, or review or collection of an account of, the consumer; or

    (B) intends to use the information for employment purposes; or

(C) intends to use the information in connection with the underwriting of insurance involving the consumer; or

(D) intends to use the information in connection with a determination of the consumer's eligibility for a license or other benefit granted by a governmental instrumentality required by law to consider an applicant's financial responsibility or status; or

(E) intends to use the information, as a potential investor or servicer, or current insurer, in connection with a valuation of, or an assessment of the credit or prepayment risks associated with, an existing credit obligation; or

(F) otherwise has a legitimate business need for the information
  (i) in connection with a business transaction that is initiated by the consumer; or
  (ii) to review an account to determine whether the consumer continues to meet the terms of the account.

(b) Conditions for furnishing and using consumer reports for employment purposes.
  (1) Certification from user.

  A consumer reporting agency may furnish a consumer report for employment purposes only if

  (A) the person who obtains such report from the agency certifies to the agency that
    (i) the person has complied with paragraph (2) with respect to the consumer report, and the person will comply with paragraph (3) with respect to the consumer report if paragraph (3) becomes applicable; and
    (ii) information from the consumer report will not be used in violation of any applicable Federal or State equal employment opportunity law or regulation; and

  (B) the consumer reporting agency provides with the report a summary of the consumer's rights under this subchapter, as prescribed by the Federal Trade Commission under section 1681g(c)(3) of this title.

  (2) Disclosure to consumer.

  A person may not procure a consumer report, or cause a consumer report to be procured, for employment purposes with respect to any consumer, unless

  (A) a clear and conspicuous disclosure has been made in writing to the consumer at any time before the report is procured or caused to be procured, in a document that consists solely of the disclosure, that a consumer report may be obtained for employment purposes; and

  (B) the consumer has authorized in writing the procurement of the report by that person.

(3) Conditions on use for adverse actions.

In using a consumer report for employment purposes, before taking any adverse action based in whole or in part on the report, the person intending to take such adverse action shall provide to the consumer to whom the report relates

(A) a copy of the report; and

(B) a description in writing of the rights of the consumer under this subchapter, as prescribed by the Federal Trade Commission under section 1681g(c)(3) of this title.

(c) Furnishing reports in connection with credit or insurance transactions that are not initiated by the consumer.

(1) In general.

A consumer reporting agency may furnish a consumer report relating to any consumer pursuant to subparagraph (A) or (C) of subsection (a) (3) of this section in connection with any credit or insurance transaction that is not initiated by the consumer only if

(A) the consumer authorizes the agency to provide such report to such person; or

(B)(i) the transaction consists of a firm offer of credit or insurance

(ii) the consumer reporting agency has complied with subsection (e) of this section; and

(iii) there is not in effect an election by the consumer, made in accordance with subsection (e) of this section, to have the consumer's name and address excluded from lists of names provided by the agency pursuant to this paragraph.

(2) Limits on information received in paragraph (1)(B).

A person may receive pursuant to paragraph (1)(B) only

(A) the name and address of a consumer;

(B) an identifier that is not unique to the consumer and that is used by the person solely for the purpose of verifying the identity of the consumer; and

(C) other information pertaining to a consumer that does not identify the relationship or experience of the consumer with respect to a particular creditor or other entity

(3) Information regarding inquiries.

Except as provided in section 1681g(a)(5) of this title, a consumer reporting agency shall not furnish to any person a record of inquiries in connection with a credit or insurance transaction that is not initiated by a consumer.

(d) Reserved

(e) Election of consumer to be excluded from lists.

(1) In general.

A consumer may elect to have the consumer's name and address excluded from any list provided by a consumer reporting agency under subsection (c)(1)(B) of this section in connection with a credit or insurance transaction that is not initiated by the consumer, by notifying the agency in accordance with paragraph (2) that the consumer does not consent to any use of a consumer report relating to the consumer in connection with any credit or insurance transaction that is not initiated by the consumer.

(2) Manner of Notification.

A consumer shall notify a consumer reporting agency under paragraph (1)

(A) through the notification system maintained by the agency under paragraph (5); or

(B) by submitting to the agency a signed notice of election form issued by the agency for purposes of this subparagraph.

(3) Response of agency after notification through system.

Upon receipt of notification of the election of a consumer under paragraph (1) through the notification system maintained by the agency under paragraph (5), a consumer reporting agency shall

(A) inform the consumer that the election is effective only for the 2-year period following the election if the consumer does not submit to the agency a signed notice of election form issued by the agency for purposes of paragraph (2)(B); and

(B) provide to the consumer a notice of election form, if requested by the consumer, not later than 5 business days after receipt of the notification of the election through the system established under paragraph (5), in the case of a request made at the time the consumer provides notification through the system.

(4) Effectiveness of election.

An election of a consumer under paragraph (1)

(A) shall be effective with respect to a consumer reporting agency beginning 5 business days after the date on which the consumer notifies the agency in accordance with paragraph (2);

(B) shall be effective with respect to a consumer reporting agency

(i) subject to subparagraph (C), during the 2-year period beginning 5 business days after the date on which the consumer notifies the agency of the election, in the case of an election for which a consumer notifies the agency only in accordance with paragraph (2)(A); or

(ii) until the consumer notifies the agency under subparagraph (C), in the case of an election for which a consumer notifies the agency in accordance with paragraph (2)(B);

(C) shall not be effective after the date on which the consumer notifies the agency, through the notification system established by the agency under paragraph (5), that the election is no longer effective; and

(D) shall be effective with respect to each affiliate of the agency.

(5) Notification system.

(A) In general.

Each consumer reporting agency that, under subsection (c)(1)(B) of this section, furnishes a consumer report in connection with a credit or insurance transaction that is not initiated by a consumer, shall

(i) establish and maintain a notification system, including a toll-free telephone number, which permits any consumer whose consumer report in maintained by the agency to notify the agency, with appropriate identification, of the consumer's election to have the consumer's name and address excluded from any such list of names and addresses provided by the agency for such a transaction; and

(ii) publish by not later than 365 days after September 30, 1996, and not less than annually thereafter, in a publication of general circulation in the area served by the agency

(I) a notification that information in consumer files maintained by the agency may be used in connection with such transactions; and

(II) the address and toll-free number for consumers to use to notify the agency of the consumer's election under clause (i).

(B) Establishment and maintenance as compliance.

Establishment and maintenance of a notification system (including a toll-free telephone number) and publication by a consumer reporting agency on the agency's own behalf and on behalf of any of its affiliates in accordance with this paragraph is deemed to be compliance with this paragraph by each of those affiliates.

(6) Notification system by agencies that operate nationwide.

Each consumer reporting agency that compiles and maintains files on consumers on a nationwide basis shall establish and maintain a notification system for purposes of paragraph (5) jointly with other such consumer reporting agencies.

(f) Certain use or obtaining of information prohibited.

A person shall not use or obtain a consumer report for any purpose unless

(1) the consumer report is obtained for a purpose for which the consumer report is authorized to be furnished under this section; and

(2) the purpose is certified in accordance with section 1681e of this title by a prospective user of the report through a general or specific certification.

(g) Furnishing reports containing medical information.

A consumer reporting agency shall not furnish for employment purposes, or in connection with a credit or insurance transaction or a direct marketing transaction, a consumer report that contains medical information about a consumer, unless the consumer consents to the furnishing of the report.

§ 1681c. Reporting of obsolete information prohibited

(a) Except as authorized under subsection (b) of this section, no consumer reporting agency may make any consumer report containing any of the following items of information:

(1) Cases under Title 11 or under the Bankruptcy Act that, from the date of entry of the order for relief or the date of adjudication, as the case may be, antedate the report by more than 10 years.

(2) Suits and judgments which, from date of entry, antedate the report by more than seven years or until the governing statute of limitations has expired, whichever is the longer period.

(3) Paid tax liens which, from date of payment, antedate the report by more than seven years.

(4) Accounts placed for collection or charged to profit and loss which antedate the report by more than seven years.

(5) Records of arrest, indictment, or conviction of crime which, from date of disposition, release, or parole, antedate the report by more than seven years.

(6) Any other adverse item of information which antedates the report by more than seven years.

(b) The provisions of subsection (a) of this section are not applicable in the case of any consumer credit report to be used in connection with—

(1) a credit transaction involving, or which may reasonably be expected to involve, a principal amount of $50,000 or more;

(2) the underwriting of life insurance involving, or which may reasonably be expected to involve, a face amount of $50,000 or more; or

(3) the employment of any individual at an annual salary which equals, or which may reasonably be expected to equal $20,000, or more.

§ 1681d. Disclosure of investigative consumer reports

(a) Disclosure of fact of preparation

A person may not procure or cause to be prepared an investigative consumer report on any consumer unless—

(1) it is clearly and accurately disclosed to the consumer that an investigative consumer report including information as to his character, general reputation, personal characteristics, and mode of living, whichever are applicable, may be made, and such disclosure

(A) is made in a writing mailed, or otherwise delivered, to the consumer, not later than three days after the date on which the report was first requested; and

(B) includes a statement informing the consumer of his right to request the additional disclosures provided for under subsection (b) of this section and the written summary of the rights of the consumer prepared pursuant to section 1681g(c) of this title; and

(2) the person certifies or has certified to the consumer reporting agency that

(A) the person has made the disclosures to the consumer required by paragraph (1); and

(B) the person will comply with subsection (b) of this section.

(b) Disclosure on request of nature and scope of investigation.

Any person who procures or causes to be prepared an investigative consumer report on any consumer shall, upon written request made by the consumer within a reasonable period of time after the receipt by him of the disclosure required by subsection (a)(1) of this section, [FN1] make a complete and accurate disclosure of the nature and scope of the investigation requested. This disclosure shall be made in a writing mailed, or otherwise delivered, to the consumer not later than five days after the date on which the request for such disclosure was received from the consumer or such report was first requested, whichever is the later.

(c) Limitation on liability upon showing of reasonable procedures for compliance with provisions.

No person may be held liable for any violation of subsection (a) or (b) of this section if he shows by a preponderance of the evidence that at the time of the violation he maintained reasonable procedures to assure compliance with subsection (a) or (b) of this section.

(d) Prohibitions.

(1) Certification.

A consumer reporting agency shall not prepare or furnish an investigative consumer report unless the agency has received a certification under subsection (a)(2) of this section from the person who requested the report.

(2) Inquiries.

A consumer reporting agency shall not make an inquiry for the purpose of preparing an investigative consumer report on a consumer for employment purposes if the making of the inquiry by an employer or prospective employer of the consumer would violate any applicable Federal or State equal employment opportunity law or regulation.

(3) Certain public record information.

Except as otherwise provided in section 1681k of this title, a consumer reporting agency shall not furnish an investigative consumer report that includes information that is a matter of public record and that relates to an arrest, indictment, conviction, civil judicial action, tax lien, or outstanding judgment, unless the agency has verified the accuracy of the information during the 30-day period ending on the date on which the report is furnished.

(4) Certain adverse information.

A consumer reporting agency shall not prepare or furnish an investigative consumer report on a consumer that contains information that is adverse to the interest of the consumer and that is obtained through a personal interview with a neighbor, friend, or associate of the consumer or with another person with whom the consumer is acquainted or who has knowledge of such item of information, unless

(A) the agency has followed reasonable procedures to obtain confirmation of the information, from an additional source that has independent and direct knowledge of the information; or

(B) the person interviewed is the best possible source of the information.

§ 1681e. Compliance procedures

(a) Identity and purpose of credit users.

Every consumer reporting agency shall maintain reasonable procedures designed to avoid violations of section 1681c of this title and to limit the furnishing of consumer reports to the purposes listed under section 1681b of this title. These procedures shall require that prospective users of the information identify themselves, certify the purposes for which the information is sought, and certify that the information will be used for no other purpose. Every consumer reporting agency shall make a reasonable effort to verify the identity of a new prospective user and the uses certified by such prospective user prior to furnishing such user a consumer report. No consumer reporting agency may furnish a consumer report to any person if it has reasonable grounds for believing that the consumer report will not be used for a purpose listed in section 1681b of this title.

(b) Accuracy of report.

Whenever a consumer reporting agency prepares a consumer report it shall follow reasonable procedures to assure maximum possible accuracy of the information concerning the individual about whom the report relates.

(c) Disclosure of consumer reports by users allowed.

A consumer reporting agency may not prohibit a user of a consumer report furnished by the agency on a consumer from disclosing the contents of the report to the consumer, if adverse action against the consumer has been taken by the user based in whole or in part on the report.

(d) Notice to users and furnishers of information.

(1) Notice requirement.

A consumer reporting agency shall provide to any person

    (A) who regularly and in the ordinary course of business furnishes information to the agency with respect to any consumer; or

    (B) to whom a consumer report is provided by the agency;

a notice of such person's responsibilities under this subchapter.

(2) Content of notice.

The Federal Trade Commission shall prescribe the content of notices under paragraph (1), and a consumer reporting agency shall be in compliance with this subsection if it provides a notice under paragraph (1) that is substantially similar to the Federal Trade Commission prescription under this paragraph.

(e) Procurement of consumer report for resale.

(1) Disclosure.

A person may not procure a consumer report for purposes of reselling the report (or any information in the report) unless the person discloses to the consumer reporting agency that originally furnishes the report

    (A) the identity of the end-user of the report (or information); and

    (B) each permissible purpose under section 1681b of this title for which the report is furnished to the end-user of the report (or information).

(2) Responsibilities of procurers for resale.

A person who procures a consumer report for purposes of reselling the report (or any information in the report) shall

    (A) establish and comply with reasonable procedures designed to ensure that the report (or information) is resold by the person only for a purpose for which the report may be furnished under section 1681b of this title, including by requiring that each person to which the report (or information) is resold and that resells or provides the report (or information) to any other person

        (i) identifies each end user of the resold report (or information);

        (ii) certifies each purpose for which the report (or information) will be used; and

        (iii) certifies that the report (or information) will be used for no other purpose; and

    (B) before reselling the report, make reasonable efforts to verify the identifications and certifications made under subparagraph (A).

§ 1681f. Disclosures to governmental agencies

Notwithstanding the provisions of section 1681b of this title, a consumer reporting agency may furnish identifying information respecting any consumer, limited to his name, address, former addresses, places of employment, or former places of employment, to a governmental agency.

§ 1681g. Disclosures to consumers

(a) Information on file; sources; report recipients

Every consumer reporting agency shall, upon request and proper identification of any consumer, clearly and accurately disclose to the consumer:

(1) The nature and substance of all information (except medical information) in its files on the consumer at the time of the request.

(2) The sources of the information; except that the sources of information acquired solely for use in preparing an investigative consumer report and actually used for no other purpose need not be disclosed: Provided, That in the event an action is brought under this subchapter, such sources shall be available to the plaintiff under appropriate discovery procedures in the court in which the action is brought.

(3) The recipients of any consumer report on the consumer which it has furnished

(A) Identification of each person (including each end-user identified under section 1681e(e)(1) of this title) that procured a consumer report

(i) for employment purposes, during the 2-year period preceding the date on which the request is made; or

(ii) for any other purpose, during the 1-year period preceding the date on which the request is made.

(B) An identification of a person under subparagraph (A) shall include

(i) the name of the person or, if applicable, the trade name (written in full) under which such person conducts business; and

(ii) upon request of the consumer, the address and telephone number of the person.

(4) The dates, original payees, and amounts of any checks upon which is based any adverse characterization of the consumer, included in the file at the time of the disclosure.

(5) A record of all inquiries received by the agency during the 1-year period preceding the request that identified the consumer in connection with a credit or insurance transaction that was not initiated by the consumer.

(b) Exempt information.

The requirements of subsection (a) of this section respecting the disclosure of sources of information and the recipients of consumer reports do not apply to information received or consumer reports furnished prior to the effective date of this subchapter except to the extent that the matter involved is contained in the files of the consumer reporting agency on that date.

(c) Summary of rights required to be included with disclosure.

(1) Summary of rights.

A consumer reporting agency shall provide to a consumer, with each written disclosure by the agency to the consumer under this section

(A) a written summary of all of the rights that the consumer has under this subchapter; and

(B) in the case of a consumer reporting agency that compiles and maintains files on consumers on a nationwide basis, a toll-free telephone number established by the agency, at which personnel are accessible to consumers during normal business hours.

(2) Specific items required to be included.

The summary of rights required under paragraph (1) shall include

(A) a brief description of this subchapter and all rights of consumers under this subchapter;

(B) an explanation of how the consumer may exercise the rights of the consumer under this subchapter;

(C) a list of all Federal agencies responsible for enforcing any provision of this subchapter and the address and any appropriate phone number of each such agency, in a form that will assist the consumer in selecting the appropriate agency;

(D) a statement that the consumer may have additional rights under State law and that the consumer may wish to contact a State or local consumer protection agency or a State attorney general to learn of those rights; and

(E) a statement that a consumer reporting agency is not required to remove accurate derogatory information from a consumer's file, unless the information is outdated under section 1681c of this title or cannot be verified.

(3) Form of summary of rights.

For purposes of this subsection and any disclosure by a consumer reporting agency required under this subchapter with respect to consumers' rights, the Federal Trade Commission (after consultation with each Federal agency referred to in section 1681s(b) of this title) shall prescribe the form and content of any such disclosure of the rights of consumers required under this subchapter. A consumer reporting agency shall be in compliance with this subsection if it provides disclosures under paragraph (1) that are substantially similar to the Federal Trade Commission prescription under this paragraph.

(4) Effectiveness.

No disclosures shall be required under this subsection until the date on which the Federal Trade Commission prescribes the form and content of such disclosures under paragraph (3).

§ 1681h. Conditions and form of disclosure to consumers

(a) In general.

(1) Proper identification.

A consumer reporting agency shall require, as a condition of making the disclosures required under section 1681g of this title, that the consumer furnish proper identification.

(2) Disclosure in writing.

Except as provided in subsection (b) of this section, the disclosures required to be made under section 1681(g) of this title shall be provided under that section in writing.

(b) Other forms of disclosure.

(1) In general.

If authorized by a consumer, a consumer reporting agency may make the disclosures required under 1681g of this title

(A) other than in writing; and

(B) in such form as may be

(i) specified by the consumer in accordance with paragraph (2); and

(ii) available from the agency.

(2) Form.

A consumer may specify pursuant to paragraph (1) that disclosures under section 1681g of this title shall be made

(A) in person, upon the appearance of the consumer at the place of business of the consumer reporting agency where disclosures are regularly provided, during normal business hours, and on reasonable notice;

(B) by telephone, if the consumer has made a written request for disclosure by telephone;

(C) by electronic means, if available from the agency; or

(D) by any other reasonable means that is available from the agency.

(c) Trained personnel

Any consumer reporting agency shall provide trained personnel to explain to the consumer any information furnished to him pursuant to section 1681g of this title.

(d) Persons accompanying consumer

The consumer shall be permitted to be accompanied by one other person of his choosing, who shall furnish reasonable identification. A consumer reporting agency may require the consumer to furnish a written statement granting permission to the consumer reporting agency to discuss the consumer's file in such person's presence.

(e) Limitation of liability

Except as provided in sections 1681n and 1681o of this title, no consumer may bring any action or proceeding in the nature of defamation, invasion of privacy, or negligence with respect to the reporting of information against any consumer reporting agency, any user of information, or any person who furnishes information to a consumer reporting agency, based on information disclosed pursuant to section 1681g, 1681h, or 1681m of this title, or based on information disclosed by a user of a consumer report to or for a consumer against whom the user has taken adverse action, based in whole or in part on the report, except as to false information furnished with malice or willful intent to injure such consumer.

§ 1681i. Procedure in case of disputed accuracy

(a) Reinvestigations of disputed information.

(1) Reinvestigation required.

(A) In general.

If the completeness or accuracy of any item of information contained in a consumer's file at a consumer reporting agency is disputed by the consumer and the consumer notifies the agency directly of such dispute, the agency shall reinvestigate free of charge and record the current status of the disputed information, or delete the item from the file in accordance with paragraph (5), before the end of the 30-day period beginning on the date on which the agency receives the notice of the dispute from the consumer.

(B) Extension of period to reinvestigate.

Except as provided in subparagraph (C), the 30-day period described in subparagraph (A) may be extended for not more than 15 additional days if the consumer reporting agency receives information from the consumer during that 30-day period that is relevant to the reinvestigation.

(C) Limitations on extension of period to reinvestigate.

Subparagraph (B) shall not apply to any reinvestigation in which, during the 30-day period described in subparagraph (A), the information that is the subject of the reinvestigation is found to be inaccurate or incomplete or the consumer reporting agency determines that the information cannot be verified.

(2) Prompt notice of dispute to furnisher of information.

(A) In general.

Before the expiration of the 5-business-day period

beginning on the date on which a consumer reporting agency receives notice of a dispute from any consumer in accordance with paragraph (1), the agency shall provide notification of the dispute to any person who provided any item of information in dispute, at the address and in the manner established with the person. The notice shall include all relevant information regarding the dispute that the agency has received from the consumer.

(B) Provision of other information from consumer.

The consumer reporting agency shall promptly provide to the person who provided the information in dispute all relevant information regarding the dispute that is received by the agency from the consumer after the period referred to in subparagraph (A) and before the end of the period referred to in paragraph (1)(A).

(3) Determination that dispute is frivolous or irrelevant.

(A) In general.

Notwithstanding paragraph (1), a consumer reporting agency may terminate a reinvestigation of information disputed by a consumer under that paragraph if the agency reasonably determines that the dispute by the consumer is frivolous or irrelevant, including by reason of a failure by a consumer to provide sufficient information to investigate the disputed information.

(B) Notice of determination.

Upon making any determination in accordance with subparagraph (A) that a dispute is frivolous or irrelevant, a consumer reporting agency shall notify the consumer of such determination not later than 5 business days after making such determination, by mail or, if authorized by the consumer for that purpose, by any other means available to the agency.

(C) Contents of notice.

A notice under subparagraph (B) shall include

(i) the reasons for the determination under subparagraph (A); and

(ii) identification of any information required to investigate the disputed information, which may consist of a standardized form describing the general nature of such information.

(4) Consideration of consumer information.

In conducting any reinvestigation under paragraph (1) with respect to disputed information in the file of any consumer, the consumer reporting agency shall review and consider all relevant information submitted by the consumer in the period described in paragraph (1)(A) with respect to such disputed information.

(5) Treatment of inaccurate or unverifiable information.

(A) In general.

If, after any reinvestigation under paragraph (1) of any information disputed by a consumer, an item of the information is found to be inaccurate or incomplete or cannot be verified, the consumer reporting agency shall promptly delete that item of information from the consumer's file or modify that item of information, as appropriate, based on the results of the reinvestigation.

(B) Requirements relating to reinsertion of previously deleted material.

(i) Certification of accuracy of information.

If any information is deleted from a consumer's file pursuant to subparagraph (A), the information may not be reinserted in the file by the consumer reporting agency unless the person who furnishes the information certifies that the information is complete and accurate.

(ii) Notice to consumer.

If any information that has been deleted from a consumer's file pursuant to subparagraph (A) is reinserted in the file, the consumer reporting agency shall notify the consumer of the reinsertion in writing not later than 5 business days after the reinsertion or, if authorized by the consumer for that purpose, by any other means available to the agency.

(iii) Additional information.

As part of, or in addition to, the notice under clause (ii), a consumer reporting agency shall provide to a consumer in writing not later than 5 business days after the date of the reinsertion

(I) a statement that the disputed information has been reinserted;

(II) the business name and address of any furnisher of information contacted and the telephone number of such furnisher, if reasonably available, or of any furnisher of information that contacted the consumer reporting agency, in connection with the reinsertion of such information; and

(III) a notice that the consumer has the right to add a statement to the consumer's file disputing the accuracy or completeness of the disputed information.

(C) Procedures to prevent reappearance.

A consumer reporting agency shall maintain reasonable procedures designed to prevent the reappearance in a consumer's file, and in consumer reports on the consumer, of information that is deleted pursuant to this paragraph (other than information that is reinserted in accordance with subparagraph (B)(i)).

(D) Automated reinvestigation system.

Any consumer reporting agency that compiles and maintains files on consumers on a nationwide basis shall implement an automated system through which furnishers of information to that consumer reporting agency may report the results of a reinvestigation that finds incomplete or inaccurate information in a consumer's file to other such consumer reporting agencies.

(6) Notice of results of reinvestigation.

(A) In general.

A consumer reporting agency shall provide written notice to a consumer of the results of a reinvestigation under this subsection not later than 5 business days after the completion of the reinvestigation, by mail or, if authorized by the consumer for that purpose, by other means available to the agency.

(B) Contents.

As part of, or in addition to, the notice under subparagraph (A), a consumer reporting agency shall provide to a consumer in writing before the expiration of the 5-day period referred to in subparagraph (A)

(i) a statement that the reinvestigation is completed;

(ii) a consumer report that is based upon the consumer's file as that file is revised as a result of the reinvestigation;

(iii) a notice that, if requested by the consumer, a description of the procedure used to determine the accuracy and completeness of the information shall be provided to the consumer by the agency, including the business name and address of any furnisher of information contacted in connection with such information and the telephone number of such furnisher, if reasonably available;

(iv) a notice that the consumer has the right to add a statement to the consumer's file disputing the accuracy or completeness of the information; and

(v) a notice that the consumer has the right to request

under subsection (d) of this section that the consumer reporting agency furnish notifications under that subsection.

(7) Description of reinvestigation procedure.

A consumer reporting agency shall provide to a consumer a description referred to in paragraph (6)(B)(iv) by not later than 15 days after receiving a request from the consumer for that description.

(8) Expedited dispute resolution.

If a dispute regarding an item of information in a consumer's file at a consumer reporting agency is resolved in accordance with paragraph (5)(A) by the deletion of the disputed information by not later than 3 business days after the date on which the agency receives notice of the dispute from the consumer in accordance with paragraph (1)(A), then the agency shall not be required to comply with paragraphs (2), (6), and (7) with respect to that dispute if the agency

(A) provides prompt notice of the deletion to the consumer by telephone;

(B) includes in that notice, or in a written notice that accompanies a confirmation and consumer report provided in accordance with subparagraph (C), a statement of the consumer's right to request under subsection (d) of this section that the agency furnish notifications under that subsection; and

(C) provides written confirmation of the deletion and a copy of a consumer report on the consumer that is based on the consumer's file after the deletion, not later than 5 business days after making the deletion. ·

(b) Statement of dispute

If the reinvestigation does not resolve the dispute, the consumer may file a brief statement setting forth the nature of the dispute. The consumer reporting agency may limit such statements to not more than one hundred words if it provides the consumer with assistance in writing a clear summary of the dispute.

(c) Notification of consumer dispute in subsequent consumer reports

Whenever a statement of a dispute is filed, unless there is reasonable grounds to believe that it is frivolous or irrelevant, the consumer reporting agency shall, in any subsequent consumer report containing the information in question, clearly note that it is disputed by the consumer and provide either the consumer's statement or a clear and accurate codification or summary thereof.

(d) Notification of deletion of disputed information

Following any deletion of information which is found to be inaccurate or whose accuracy can no longer be verified or any notation as to disputed information, the consumer reporting agency shall, at the request of the consumer, furnish notification that the item has been deleted or the statement, codification or summary pursuant to subsection (b) or (c) of this section to any person specifically designated by the consumer who has within two years prior thereto received a consumer report for employment purposes, or within six months prior thereto received a consumer report for any other purpose, which contained the deleted or disputed information.

§ 1681j. Charges for disclosures

(a) Reasonable charges allowed for certain disclosures

(1) In general.

Except as provided in subsections (b), (c), and (d) of this section, a consumer reporting agency may impose a reasonable charge on a consumer

(A) for making a disclosure to the consumer pursuant to section 1681g of this title, which charge

(i) shall not exceed $8; and

(ii) shall be indicated to the consumer before making the disclosure; and

(B) for furnishing, pursuant to section 1681i(d) of this title, following a reinvestigation under section 1681i(a) of this title, a statement, codification, or summary to a person designated by the consumer under that section after the 30-day period beginning on the date of notification of the consumer under paragraph (6) or (8) of section 1681i(a) of this title with respect to the reinvestigation, which charge

(i) shall not exceed the charge that the agency would impose on each designated recipient for a consumer report; and

(ii) shall be indicated to the consumer before furnishing such information.

(2) Modification of amount.

The Federal Trade Commission shall increase the amount referred to in paragraph (1)(A)(i) on January 1 of each year, based proportionally on changes in the Consumer Price Index, with fractional changes rounded to the nearest fifty cents.

(b) Free disclosure after adverse notice to consumer.

Each consumer reporting agency that maintains a file on a consumer shall make all disclosures pursuant to section 1681g of this title without charge to the consumer if, not later than 60 days after receipt by such consumer of a notification pursuant to section 1681m of this title, or of a notification from a debt collection agency affiliated with that consumer reporting agency stating that the consumer's credit rating may be or has been adversely affected, the consumer makes a request under section 1681g of this title.

(c) Free disclosure under certain other circumstances.

Upon the request of the consumer, a consumer reporting agency shall make all disclosures pursuant to section 1681g of this title once during any 12- month period without charge to that consumer if the consumer certifies in writing that the consumer

(1) is unemployed and intends to apply for employment in the 60-day period beginning on the date on which the certification is made;

(2) is a recipient of public welfare assistance; or

(3) has reason to believe that the file on the consumer at the agency contains inaccurate information due to fraud.

(d) Other charges prohibited.

A consumer reporting agency shall not impose any charge on a consumer for providing any notification required by this subchapter or making any disclosure required by this subchapter, except as authorized by subsection (a) of this section.

§ 1681k. Public record information for employment purposes

A consumer reporting agency which furnishes a consumer report for employment purposes and which for that purpose compiles and reports items of information on consumers which are matters of public record and are likely to have an adverse effect upon a consumer's ability to obtain employment shall—

(1) at the time such public record information is reported to the user of such consumer report, notify the consumer of the fact that public record information is being reported by the consumer reporting agency, together with the name and address of the person to whom such information is being reported; or

(2) maintain strict procedures designed to insure that whenever public record information which is likely to have an adverse effect on a consumer's ability to obtain employment is reported it is complete and up to date. For purposes of this paragraph, items of public record relating to arrests, indictments, convictions, suits, tax liens, and outstanding judgments shall be considered up to date if the current public record status of the item at the time of the report is reported.

§ 1681l. Restrictions on investigative consumer reports

Whenever a consumer reporting agency prepares an investigative consumer report, no adverse information in the consumer report (other than information which is a matter of public record) may be included in a subsequent consumer report unless such adverse information has been verified in the process of making such subsequent consumer report, or the adverse information was received within the three-month period preceding the date the subsequent report is furnished.

§ 1681m. Requirements on users of consumer reports

(a) Duties of users taking adverse actions on the basis of information contained in consumer reports.

If any person takes any adverse action with respect to any consumer that is based in whole or in part on any information contained in a consumer report, the person shall

(1) provide oral, written, or electronic notice of the adverse action to the consumer;

(2) provide to the consumer orally, in writing, or electronically

  (A) the name, address, and telephone number of the consumer reporting agency (including a toll-free telephone number established by the agency if the agency compiles and maintains files on consumers on a nationwide basis) that furnished the report to the person; and

  (B) a statement that the consumer reporting agency did not make the decision to take the adverse action and is unable to provide the consumer the specific reasons why the adverse action was taken; and

(3) provide to the consumer an oral, written, or electronic notice of the consumer's right

  (A) to obtain, under section 1681j of this title, a free copy of a consumer report on the consumer from the consumer reporting agency referred to in paragraph (2), which notice shall include an indication of the 60-day period under that section for obtaining such a copy; and

  (B) to dispute, under section 1681i of this title, with a consumer reporting agency the accuracy or completeness of any information in a consumer report furnished by the agency.

(b) Adverse action based on information obtained from third parties other than consumer reporting agencies.

(1) In general.

Whenever credit for personal, family, or household purposes involving a consumer is denied or the charge for such credit is increased either wholly or partly because of information obtained from a person other than a consumer reporting agency bearing upon the consumer's credit worthiness, credit standing, credit capacity, character, general reputation, personal characteristics, or mode of living, the user of such information shall, within a reasonable period of time, upon the consumer's written request for the reasons for such adverse action received within sixty days after learning of such adverse action, disclose the nature of the information to the consumer. The user of such information shall clearly and accurately disclose to the consumer his right to make such written request at the time such adverse action is communicated to the consumer.

(2) Duties of person taking certain actions based on information provided by affiliate.

  (A) Duties, generally.

    If a person takes an action described in subparagraph (B) with respect to a consumer, based in whole or in part on information described in subparagraph (C), the person shall

    (i) notify the consumer of the action, including a

statement that the consumer may obtain the information in accordance with clause (ii); and

(ii) upon a written request from the consumer received within 60 days after transmittal of the notice required by clause (i), disclose to the consumer the nature of the information upon which the action is based by not later than 30 days after receipt of the request.

(B) Action described.

An action referred to in subparagraph (A) is an adverse action described in section 1681a(k)(1)(A) of this title, taken in connection with a transaction initiated by the consumer, or any adverse action described in clause (i) or (ii) of section 1681(k)(1)(B) of this title.

(C) Information described.

Information referred to in subparagraph (A)

(i) except as provided in clause (ii), is information that

(I) is furnished to the person taking the action by a person related by common ownership or affiliated by common corporate control to the person taking the action; and

(II) bears on the credit worthiness, credit standing, credit capacity, character, general reputation, personal characteristics, or mode of living of the consumer; and

(ii) does not include

(I) information solely as to transactions or experiences between the consumer and the person furnishing the information; or

(II) information in a consumer report.

(c) Reasonable procedures to assure compliance

No person shall be held liable for any violation of this section if he shows by a preponderance of the evidence that at the time of the alleged violation he maintained reasonable procedures to assure compliance with the provisions of this section.

(d) Duties of users making written credit or insurance solicitations on the basis of information contained in consumer files.

(1) In general.

Any person who uses a consumer report on any consumer in connection with any credit or insurance transaction that is not initiated by the consumer, that is provided to that person under section 1681b(c)(1)(B) of this title, shall provide with each written solicitation made to the consumer regarding the transaction a clear and conspicuous statement that

(A) information contained in the consumer's consumer report was used in connection with the transaction;

(B) the consumer received the offer of credit or insurance because the consumer satisfied the criteria for credit worthiness or insurability under which the consumer was selected for the offer;

(C) if applicable, the credit or insurance may not be extended if, after the consumer responds to the offer, the consumer does not meet the criteria used to select the consumer for the offer or any applicable criteria bearing on credit worthiness or insurability or does not furnish any required collateral;

(D) the consumer has a right to prohibit information contained in the consumer's file with any consumer reporting agency from being used in connection with any credit or insurance transaction that is not initiated by the consumer; and

(E) the consumer may exercise the right referred to in subparagraph (D) by notifying a notification system established under section 1681b(e) of this title.

(2) Disclosure of address and telephone number.

A statement under paragraph (1) shall include the address and toll-free telephone number of the appropriate notification system established under section 1681b(e) of this title.

(3) Maintaining criteria on file.

A person who makes an offer of credit or insurance to a consumer under a credit or insurance transaction described in paragraph (1) shall maintain on file the criteria used to select the consumer to receive the offer, all criteria bearing on credit worthiness or insurability, as applicable, that are the basis for determining whether or not to extend credit or insurance pursuant to the offer, and any requirement for the furnishing of collateral as a condition of the extension of credit or insurance, until the expiration of the 3-year period beginning on the date on which the offer is made to the consumer.

(4) Authority of Federal agencies regarding unfair or deceptive acts or practices not affected.

This section is not intended to affect the authority of any Federal or State agency to enforce a prohibition against unfair or deceptive acts or practices, including the making of false or misleading statements in connection with a credit or insurance transaction that is not initiated by the consumer.

§ 1681n. Civil liability for willful noncompliance

(a) In general.

Any person who willfully fails to comply with any requirement imposed under this subchapter with respect to any consumer is liable to that consumer in an amount equal to the sum of

(1) (A) any actual damages sustained by the consumer as a result of the failure or damages of not less than $100 and not more than $1,000; or

(B) in the case of liability of a natural person for obtaining a consumer report under false pretenses or knowingly without a permissible purpose, actual damages sustained by the consumer as a result of the failure of $1,000, whichever is greater;

(2) such amount of punitive damages as the court may allow; and

(3) in the case of any successful action to enforce any liability under this section, the costs of the action together with reasonable attorney's fees as determined by the court.

(b) Civil liability for knowing noncompliance.

Any person who obtains a consumer report from a consumer reporting agency under false pretenses or knowingly without a permissible purpose shall be liable to the consumer reporting agency for actual damages sustained by the consumer reporting agency or $1,000, whichever is greater.

(c) Attorney's fees.

Upon a finding by the court that an unsuccessful pleading, motion, or other paper filed in connection with an action under this section was filed in bad faith or for purposes of harassment, the court shall award to the prevailing party attorney's fees reasonable in relation to the work expended in responding to the pleading, motion, or other paper.

§ 1681o. Civil liability for negligent noncompliance

(a) In general.

Any person who is negligent in failing to comply with any requirement imposed under this subchapter with respect to any consumer is liable to that consumer in an amount equal to the sum of

(1) any actual damages sustained by the consumer as a result of the failure;

(2) in the case of any successful action to enforce any liability under this section, the costs of the action together with reasonable attorney's fees as determined by the court.

(b) Attorney's fees.

On a finding by the court that an unsuccessful pleading, motion, or other paper filed in connection with an action under this section was filed in bad faith or for purposes of harassment, the court shall award to the prevailing party attorney's fees reasonable in relation to the work expended in responding to the pleading, motion, or other paper.

§ 1681p. Jurisdiction of courts; limitation of actions

An action to enforce any liability created under this subchapter may be brought in any appropriate United States district court without regard to the amount in controversy, or in any other court of competent jurisdiction, within two years from the date on which the liability arises, except that where a defendant has materially and willfully misrepresented any information required under this subchapter to be disclosed to an individual and the information so misrepresented is material to the establishment of the defendant's liability to that individual under this subchapter, the action may be brought at any time within two years after discovery by the individual of the misrepresentation.

§ 1681q. Obtaining information under false pretenses

Any person who knowingly and willfully obtains information on a consumer from a consumer reporting agency under false pretenses shall be fined under Title 18, imprisoned for not more than 2 years, or both.

§ 1681r. Unauthorized disclosures by officers or employees

Any officer or employee of a consumer reporting agency who knowingly and willfully provides information concerning an individual from the agency's files to a person not authorized to receive that information shall be fined under Title 18, imprisoned for not more than 2 years, or both.

§ 1681s. Administrative enforcement

(a) (1) Federal Trade Commission; powers
Enforcement by Federal Trade Commission.
Compliance with the requirements imposed under this subchapter shall be enforced under the Federal Trade Commission Act by the Federal Trade Commission with respect to consumer reporting agencies and all other persons subject thereto, except to the extent that enforcement of the requirements imposed under this subchapter is specifically committed to some other government agency under subsection (b) hereof. For the purpose of the exercise by the Federal Trade Commission of its functions and powers under the Federal Trade Commission Act, a violation of any requirement or prohibition imposed under this subchapter shall constitute an unfair or deceptive act or practice in commerce in violation of section 5(a) of the Federal Trade Commission Act and shall be subject to enforcement by the Federal Trade Commission under section 5(b) thereof with respect to any consumer reporting agency or person subject to enforcement by the Federal Trade Commission pursuant to this subsection, irrespective of whether that person is engaged in commerce or meets any other jurisdictional tests in the Federal Trade Commission Act. The Federal Trade Commission shall have such procedural, investigative, and enforcement powers, including the power to issue procedural rules in enforcing compliance with the requirements imposed under this subchapter and to require the filing of reports, the production of documents, and the appearance of witnesses as though the applicable terms and conditions of the Federal Trade Commission Act were part of this subchapter. Any person violating any of the provisions of this subchapter shall be subject to the penalties and entitled to the privileges and immunities provided in the Federal Trade Commission Act as though the applicable terms and provisions thereof were part of this

subchapter.

(2)   (A) In the event of a knowing violation, which constitutes a pattern or practice of violations of this subchapter, the Commission may commence a civil action to recover a civil penalty in a district court of the United States against any person that violates this subchapter. In such action, such person shall be liable for a civil penalty of not more than $2,500 per violation.

    (B) In determining the amount of a civil penalty under subparagraph (A), the court shall take into account the degree of culpability, any history of prior such conduct, ability to pay, effect on ability to continue to do business, and such other matters as justice may require.

(3) Notwithstanding paragraph (2), a court may not impose any civil penalty on a person for a violation of section 1681s-2(a)(1) of this title unless the person has been enjoined from committing the violation, or ordered not to commit the violation, in an action or proceeding brought by or on behalf of the Federal Trade Commission, and has violated the injunction or order, and the court may not impose any civil penalty for any violation occurring before the date of the violation of the injunction or order.

(4) Neither the Commission nor any other agency referred to in subsection (b) of this section may prescribe trade regulation rules or other regulations with respect to this subchapter.;

(b) Enforcement by other agencies.

Compliance with the requirements imposed under this subchapter with respect to consumer reporting agencies, persons who use consumer reports from such agencies, persons who furnish information to such agencies, and users of information that are subject to subsection (d) or (e) of section 1681m of this title shall be enforced under

(1) section 8 of the Federal Deposit Insurance Act [12 U.S.C.A. s 1818], in the case of—

(A) banks, and Federal branches and Federal agencies of foreign banks, by the Office of the Comptroller of the Currency;

(B) member banks of the Federal Reserve System (other than national banks), branches and agencies of foreign banks (other than Federal branches, Federal agencies, and insured State branches of foreign banks), commercial lending companies owned or controlled by foreign banks, and organizations operating under section 25 or 25(a) of the Federal Reserve Act [12 U.S.C.A. ss 601 et seq., 611 et seq.], by the Board of Governors of the Federal Reserve System; and

(C) banks insured by the Federal Deposit Insurance Corporation (other than members of the Federal Reserve System) and insured State branches of foreign banks, by the

Board of Directors of the Federal Deposit Insurance Corporation;

(2) Section 8 of the Federal Deposit Insurance Act [12 U.S.C.A. s 1818], by the Director of the Office of Thrift Supervision, in the case of a savings association the deposits of which are insured by the Federal Deposit Insurance Corporation.

(3) the Federal Credit Union Act, by the Administrator of the National Credit Union Administration with respect to any Federal credit union;

(4) subtitle IV of Title 49, by the Secretary of Transportation with respect to all carriers subject to such subtitle;

(5) the Federal Aviation Act of 1958, by the Secretary of Transportation with respect to any air carrier or foreign air carrier subject to that Act; and

(6) the Packers and Stockyards Act, 1921 (except as provided in section 406 of that Act), by the Secretary of Agriculture with respect to any activities subject to that Act.

The terms used in paragraph (1) that are not defined in this subchapter or otherwise defined in section 3(s) of the Federal Deposit Insurance Act (12 U.S.C. 1813(s)) shall have the meaning given to them in section 1(b) of the International Banking Act of 1978 (12 U.S.C. 3101).

(c) State action for violations.

(1) Authority of States.

In addition to such other remedies as are provided under State law, if the chief law enforcement officer of a State, or an official or agency designated by a State, has reason to believe that any person has violated or is violating this subchapter, the State

(A) may bring an action to enjoin such violation in any appropriate United States district court or in any other court of competent jurisdiction;

(B) subject to paragraph (5), may bring an action on behalf of the residents of the State to recover

(i) damages for which the person is liable to such residents under sections 1681n and 1681o of this title as a result of the violation;

(ii) in the case of a violation of section 1681s-2(a) of this title, damages for which the person would, but for section 1681s-2(c) of this title, be liable to such residents as a result of the violation; or

(iii) damages of not more than $1,000 for each willful or negligent violation; and

(C) in the case of any successful action under subparagraph (A) or (B), shall be awarded the costs of the action and reasonable attorney fees as determined by the court.

(2) Rights of Federal regulators.

The State shall serve prior written notice of any action under paragraph (1) upon the Federal Trade Commission or the appropriate Federal regulator determined under subsection (b) of this section and provide the Commission or appropriate Federal regulator with a copy of its complaint, except in any case in which such prior notice is not feasible, in which case the State shall serve such notice immediately upon instituting such action. The Federal Trade Commission or appropriate Federal regulator shall have the right

(A) to intervene in the action;

(B) upon so intervening, to be heard on all matters arising therein;

(C) to remove the action to the appropriate United States district court; and

(D) to file petitions for appeal.

(3) Investigatory powers.

For purposes of bringing any action under this subsection, nothing in this subsection shall prevent the chief law enforcement officer, or an official or agency designated by a State, from exercising the powers conferred on the chief law enforcement officer or such official by the laws of such State to conduct investigations or to administer oaths or affirmations or to compel the attendance of witnesses or the production of documentary and other evidence.

(4) Limitation on State action while Federal action pending.

If the Federal Trade Commission or the appropriate Federal regulator has instituted a civil action or an administrative action under section 1818 of Title 12 for a violation of this subchapter, no State may, during the pendency of such action, bring an action under this section against any defendant named in the complaint of the Commission or the appropriate Federal regulator for any violation of this subchapter that is alleged in that complaint.

(5) Limitations on State actions for violation of section 1681s-2(a)(1) of this title.

(A) Violation of injunction required.

A State may not bring an action against a person under paragraph (1)(B) for a violation of section 1681s-2(a)(1) of this title, unless

(i) the person has been enjoined from committing the violation, in an action brought by the State under paragraph (1)(A); and

(ii) the person has violated the injunction.

(B) Limitation on damages recoverable.

In an action against a person under paragraph (1)(B) for a violation of section 1681s-2(a)(1) of this title, a State may not recover any damages incurred before the date of the violation of an injunction on which the action is based."; and

(d) Enforcement under other authority

For the purpose of the exercise by any agency referred to in subsection (b) of this section of its powers under any Act referred to in that subsection, a violation of any requirement imposed under this subchapter shall be deemed to be a violation of a requirement imposed under that Act. In addition to its powers under any provision of law specifically referred to in subsection (b) of this section, each of the agencies referred to in that subsection may exercise, for the purpose of enforcing compliance with any requirement imposed under this subchapter any other authority conferred on it by law.

Notwithstanding the preceding, no agency referred to in subsection (b) of this section may conduct an examination of a bank, savings association, or credit union regarding compliance with the provisions of this subchapter, except in response to a complaint (or if the agency otherwise has knowledge) that the bank, savings association, or credit union has violated a provision of this subchapter, in which case, the agency may conduct an examination as necessary to investigate the complaint. If an agency determines during an investigation in response to a complaint that a violation of this subchapter has occurred, the agency may, during its next 2 regularly scheduled examinations of the bank, savings association, or credit union, examine for compliance with this subchapter.

(e) Interpretive authority.

The Board of Governors of the Federal Reserve System may issue interpretations of any provision of this subchapter as such provision may apply to any persons identified under paragraph (1), (2), and (3) of subsection (b) of this section, or to the holding companies and affiliates of such persons, in consultation with Federal agencies identified in paragraphs (1), (2), and (3) of subsection (b) of this section..

§ 1681s-1. Information on overdue child support obligations

Notwithstanding any other provision of this subchapter, a consumer reporting agency shall include in any consumer report furnished by the agency in accordance with section 1681b of this title, any information on the failure of the consumer to pay overdue support which—

(1) is provided—

    (A) to the consumer reporting agency by a State or local child support enforcement agency; or

    (B) to the consumer reporting agency and verified by any local, State, or Federal Government agency; and

(2) antedates the report by 7 years or less.

§ 1681t. Relation to State laws

(a) In general.

Except as provided in subsections (b) and (c) of this section, this subchapter does not annul, alter, affect, or exempt any person subject to the provisions of this subchapter from complying with the laws of any

State with respect to the collection, distribution, or use of any information on consumers, except to the extent that those laws are inconsistent with any provision of this subchapter, and then only to the extent of the inconsistency.

(b) General exceptions.

No requirement or prohibition may be imposed under the laws of any State

> (1) with respect to any subject matter regulated under
>> (A) subsection (c) or (e) of section 1681b of this title, relating to the prescreening of consumer reports;
>> (B) section 1681i of this title, relating to the time by which a consumer reporting agency must take any action, including the provision of notification to a consumer or other person, in any procedure related to the disputed accuracy of information in a consumer's file, except that this subparagraph shall not apply to any State law in effect on September 30, 1996;
>> (C) subsections (a) and (b) of section 1681m of this title, relating to the duties of a person who takes any adverse action with respect to a consumer;
>> (D) section 1681m(d) of this title, relating to the duties of persons who use a consumer report of a consumer in connection with any credit or insurance transaction that is not initiated by the consumer and that consists of a firm offer of credit or insurance;
>> (E) section 1681c of this title, relating to information contained in consumer reports, except that this subparagraph shall not apply to any State law in effect on September 30, 1996; or
>> (F) section 1681s-2 of this title, relating to the responsibilities of persons who furnish information to consumer reporting agencies, except that this paragraph shall not apply
>>> (i) with respect to section 54A(a) of chapter 93 of the Massachusetts Annotated Laws (as in effect on September 30, 1996); or
>>> (ii) with respect to section 1785.25(a) of the California Civil Code (as in effect on September 30, 1996);
> (2) with respect to the exchange of information among persons affiliated by common ownership or common corporate control, except that this paragraph shall not apply with respect to subsection (a) or (c)(1) of section 2480e of title 9, Vermont Statutes Annotated (as in effect on September 30, 1996); or
> (3) with respect to the form and content of any disclosure required to be made under section 1681g(c) of this title.

(c) Definition of firm offer of credit or insurance.—Notwithstanding any definition of the term "firm offer of credit or insurance" (or any equivalent term) under the laws of any State, the definition of that term contained in section 1681a(l) of this title shall be construed to apply in the enforcement and interpretation of the laws of any State governing consumer reports.

(d) Limitations.

Subsections (b) and (c) of this section

(1) do not affect any settlement, agreement, or consent judgment between any State Attorney General and any consumer reporting agency in effect on September 30, 1996; and

(2) do not apply to any provision of State law (including any provision of a State constitution) that

(A) is enacted after January 1, 2004;

(B) states explicitly that the provision is intended to supplement this subchapter; and

(C) gives greater protection to consumers than is provided under this subchapter.

§ 1681u. Disclosures to FBI for counterintelligence purposes

(a) Identity of financial institutions

Notwithstanding section 1681b of this title or any other provision of this subchapter, a consumer reporting agency shall furnish to the Federal Bureau of Investigation the names and addresses of all financial institutions (as that term is defined in section 3401 of Title 12) at which a consumer maintains or has maintained an account, to the extent that information is in the files of the agency, when presented with a written request for that information, signed by the Director of the Federal Bureau of Investigation, or the Director's designee, which certifies compliance with this section. The Director or the Director's designee may make such a certification only if the Director or the Director's designee has determined in writing that

(1) such information is necessary for the conduct of an authorized foreign counterintelligence investigation; and

(2) there are specific and articulable facts giving reason to believe that the consumer

(A) is a foreign power (as defined in section 1801 of Title 50) or a person who is not a United States person (as defined in such section 1801) and is an official of a foreign power; or

(B) is an agent of a foreign power and is engaging or has engaged in an act of international terrorism (as that term is defined in section 1801(c) of Title 50) or clandestine intelligence activities that involve or may involve a violation of criminal statutes of the United States.

(b) Identifying information

Notwithstanding the provisions of section 1681b of this title or any other provision of this subchapter, a consumer reporting agency shall furnish identifying information respecting a consumer, limited to name, address, former addresses, places of employment, or former places of employment, to the Federal Bureau of Investigation when presented with a written request, signed by the Director or the Director's designee, which certifies compliance with this subsection. The Director or the Director's designee may make such a certification only if the Director or the Director's designee has determined in writing that

(1) such information is necessary to the conduct of an authorized counterintelligence investigation; and

(2) there is information giving reason to believe that the consumer has been, or is about to be, in contact with a foreign power or an agent of a foreign power (as defined in section 1801 of Title 50).

(c) Court order for disclosure of consumer reports

Notwithstanding section 1681b of this title or any other provision of this subchapter, if requested in writing by the Director of the Federal Bureau of Investigation, or a designee of the Director, a court may issue an order ex parte directing a consumer reporting agency to furnish a consumer report to the Federal Bureau of Investigation, upon a showing in camera that

(1) the consumer report is necessary for the conduct of an authorized foreign counterintelligence investigation; and

(2) there are specific and articulable facts giving reason to believe that the consumer whose consumer report is sought

(A) is an agent of a foreign power, and

(B) is engaging or has engaged in an act of international terrorism (as that term is defined in section 1801(c) of Title 50) or clandestine intelligence activities that involve or may involve a violation of criminal statutes of the United States.

The terms of an order issued under this subsection shall not disclose that the order is issued for purposes of a counterintelligence investigation.

(d) Confidentiality

No consumer reporting agency or officer, employee, or agent of a consumer reporting agency shall disclose to any person, other than those officers, employees, or agents of a consumer reporting agency necessary to fulfill the requirement to disclose information to the Federal Bureau of Investigation under this section, that the Federal Bureau of Investigation has sought or obtained the identity of financial institutions or a consumer report respecting any consumer under subsection (a), (b), or (c) of this section, and no consumer reporting agency or officer, employee, or agent of a consumer reporting agency shall include in any consumer report any information that would indicate that the Federal Bureau of Investigation has sought or obtained such information or a consumer report.

(e) Payment of fees

The Federal Bureau of Investigation shall, subject to the availability of appropriations, pay to the consumer reporting agency assembling or providing report or information in accordance with procedures established under this section a fee for reimbursement for such costs as are reasonably necessary and which have been directly incurred in searching, reproducing, or transporting books, papers, records, or other data required or requested to be produced under this section.

(f) Limit on dissemination

The Federal Bureau of Investigation may not disseminate information obtained pursuant to this section outside of the Federal Bureau of Investigation, except to other Federal agencies as may be necessary for the approval or conduct of a foreign counterintelligence investigation, or, where the information concerns a person subject to the Uniform Code of Military Justice, to appropriate investigative authorities within the military department concerned as may be necessary for the conduct of a joint foreign counterintelligence investigation.

(g) Rules of construction

Nothing in this section shall be construed to prohibit information from being furnished by the Federal Bureau of Investigation pursuant to a subpoena or court order, in connection with a judicial or administrative proceeding to enforce the provisions of this subchapter. Nothing in this section shall be construed to authorize or permit the withholding of information from the Congress.

(h) Reports to Congress

On a semiannual basis, the Attorney General shall fully inform the Permanent Select Committee on Intelligence and the Committee on Banking, Finance and Urban Affairs of the House of Representatives, and the Select Committee on Intelligence and the Committee on Banking, Housing, and Urban Affairs of the Senate concerning all requests made pursuant to subsections (a), (b), and (c) of this section.

(i) Damages

Any agency or department of the United States obtaining or disclosing any consumer reports, records, or information contained therein in violation of this section is liable to the consumer to whom such consumer reports, records, or information relate in an amount equal to the sum of—

(1) $100, without regard to the volume of consumer reports, records, or information involved;

(2) any actual damages sustained by the consumer as a result of the disclosure;

(3) if the violation is found to have been willful or intentional, such punitive damages as a court may allow; and

(4) in the case of any successful action to enforce liability under this subsection, the costs of the action, together with reasonable attorney fees, as determined by the court.

(j) Disciplinary actions for violations

If a court determines that any agency or department of the United States has violated any provision of this section and the court finds that the circumstances surrounding the violation raise questions of whether or not an officer or employee of the agency or department acted willfully or intentionally with respect to the violation, the agency or department shall promptly initiate a proceeding to determine whether or not disciplinary action is warranted against the officer or employee who was responsible for the violation.

(k) Good-faith exception

Notwithstanding any other provision of this subchapter, any consumer reporting agency or agent or employee thereof making disclosure of consumer reports or identifying information pursuant to this subsection in good-faith reliance upon a certification of the Federal Bureau of Investigation pursuant to provisions of this section shall not be liable to any person for such disclosure under this subchapter, the constitution of any State, or any law or regulation of any State or any political subdivision of any State.

(l) Limitation of remedies

Notwithstanding any other provision of this subchapter, the remedies and sanctions set forth in this section shall be the only judicial remedies and sanctions for violation of this section.

(m) Injunctive relief

In addition to any other remedy contained in this section, injunctive relief shall be available to require compliance with the procedures of this section. In the event of any successful action under this subsection, costs together with reasonable attorney fees, as determined by the court, may be recovered.

Index

A-C

D-I

NOTES

NOTES

NOTES

NOTES